William Wilberforce

A Secret of the Marsh: *a story:* 1927
Uncle Lawrence: *a portrait:* 1939
Captains and Kings: *historical miniatures:* 1947
An Introduction to British Marine Painting: 1948
Joseph Conrad: *Men and Books Series:* 1951
The Crown Jewels: *King Penguin:* 1951
Captain Marryat: *a Rediscovery:* 1953
Battle Honours of the Royal Navy: 1956
A Portrait of Lord Nelson: 1958
Trafalgar: *British Battles Series:* 1959
Emma Hamilton and Sir William: 1960
The Battle of the Nile: *British Battles Series:* 1960
Great Seamen: 1961
The Glorious First of June: *British Battles Series:* 1961

I   WILLIAM WILBERFORCE
George Richmond's watercolour in the House of Commons

William Wilberforce

and his Times

OLIVER WARNER

'*Soldiers of Christ arise,*
And put your armour on . . .'
Charles Wesley

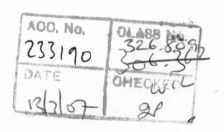

B. T. Batsford Ltd. London

First published 1962

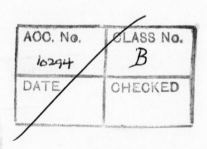

Made and printed in Great Britain
by Jarrold and Sons Ltd. London and Norwich for the publishers
B. T. BATSFORD LTD.
4 Fitzhardinge Street, Portman Square, London, W.1

To Hugh Derry

'Can you stop a cat from mousing? When I die, I shall be found with a slave in my mouth.'—*The Emir of Kontagora*

'I declare, if I could stop this traffic, I would willingly be shot this night.'—*General Gordon, on seeing a slave caravan*

(Quoted in Sir Reginald Coupland:
The British Anti-Slavery Movement: 1933)

'It requires one life to get a principle acknowledged, and another to get it acted on.'—*Benjamin Robert Haydon*

CONTENTS

ACKNOWLEDGMENT

The Author and Publishers wish to thank the following for permission to reproduce the illustrations appearing in this book:

The Trustees of the British Museum, for fig. 15.

Kingston-upon-Hull Museums, for figs. 3, 10, 11, 14 and 19.

City of Liverpool Public Libraries (Mayer Collection), for fig. 13.

The London County Council (Iveagh Bequest, Kenwood), for fig. 2.

The Ministry of Works, for fig. 1 (Crown Copyright).

The National Portrait Gallery, for figs. 4, 6–9 and 16.

The President of Queens' College, Cambridge, for fig. 5.

Josiah Wedgwood and Sons Ltd., for fig. 18.

LIST OF ILLUSTRATIONS

I   CALLING

It is sometimes good to be reminded that wrongs may be put right, and that a man may lead a noble rather than a selfish life. For centuries, the Continent of Africa was exploited in the interests of white settlements in the Americas and the West Indies. Negroes were hunted, captured alive—men, women and children alike—sold like merchandise, and transported under conditions that few animals could survive, to work till they died for people of whom they knew nothing, who trafficked in them solely because of greed for gain. It was a dreadful, protracted and shaming story, and while it lasted it was as deserving of a crusade as any cause in history.

Many Englishmen, remembered and forgotten, gave their lives to working for the abolition of this trade in human beings. One Parliamentarian, William Wilberforce (1759–1833), dedicated nearly the whole of a great public career to the cause of the slaves: more than that, he succeeded in doing what he hoped, though his mortal span was only just long enough. First he stopped the oceanic traffic in slaves by British ships: then he agitated for Emancipation of slaves in British possessions. Although he did not work alone, he was the mainspring of a fine movement, and it was his political skill, his personal gifts and charm, his enduring persistence which in the end defeated the massed and vigorous forces of vested interest and obstruction. Nearly forty years ago, Sir Reginald Coupland ended his study of Wilberforce with the following words: '. . . at midnight on 31 July 1834, eight hundred thousand slaves became free. It was more than a great event in African or in British history. It was one of the greatest events in the history of the world.'

These sentences contain no exaggeration. The longer-term effects of the Abolition of Slavery by Britain are seen on every hand today when Africa, besides being in ferment, is in process of Finding herself as a Continent, and when the whole question of racial relationships is in the forefront of politics. If Liberation was a great event a century and more ago in Britain, its importance merely began at that time. The result continues. It is still too early to see what it will be upon the pattern of the world.

The act of Liberation itself was the end of a very weary stage. No single man was responsible for the successful passing of the measure, but it is true to say that no single man did more to ensure it than William Wilberforce. That is the reason why he is remembered. Yet even Wilberforce's story, full as it is, was but a small part of a long and painful process. Although Abolition by Britain was a lead, it was many years before it was actively followed by other Powers, and it needed all the horrors of a civil war before America, supposedly the most egalitarian of countries, everywhere copied the example. Moreover, he would be innocent indeed who supposed that, even in this year of grace, slavery is an evil which has been extirpated. In some countries other names have been found for it, but it still exists.

Because, thanks to our forefathers, we have been educated to certain freedoms, it needs an unusual effort of the imagination to think back realistically to the general state of mind at the time when Wilberforce and his friends first took up the cause of the Negroes, to realise their difficulties and their persistence, and not to fall into the way of taking a later enlightenment for granted. Great names were on the side of liberation, Burke, Pitt and Fox among them, but in this respect as in others they were ahead of their age.

Any life of Wilberforce must be the study of a cause; it will be incomplete if it is not also the study of a man, one of the most engaging in the history of politics. That the cause was good, and the man both good and attractive to all who knew him well, must be accounted fortunate. It makes his story not merely a triumph of right, but an adventure in humanity. Moreover, although

Wilberforce's activities affected few events or movements confined solely to his own country, he may be accounted a maker of England in that he came to represent, to the world in general, the sort of Englishman prepared to spend his energies for the benefit of mankind at large. The idea of such a man, such a Parliamentarian, is no unworthy export, and it has helped to create an idea of England which, if perhaps it errs on the side of flattery, yet is not outrageously distorted. There is such a thing as altruism, and men like Wilberforce are proof of it.

II

In North America, the nineteenth-century struggle for the liberation of slaves was between North and South. In England, in the eighteenth century, it was between East and West. In America, it was the southern States which depended upon Negro labour for prosperity. In England, it was the western ports, first Plymouth, later Bristol and Liverpool, which most profited by what was known as the 'African Trade', though up to the middle of the eighteenth century London slave-ships formed a sizeable proportion of the tonnage employed.

As the great exponent of Abolition it was therefore appropriate that William Wilberforce should have been a native of Hull, and that throughout the most important span of his life in the House of Commons he represented his native county of Yorkshire, whose loyalty to him became famous. Wilberforce drew his wealth from the Baltic, not the African trade, and he employed it to undermine what he believed to be the iniquities from which Lancashire gained much of hers. The campaign for Abolition may therefore not unfairly be considered, in part at least, an episode in the rivalry of the white rose and the red, but it should also be remembered, to its honour, that Liverpool itself, the greatest slaving port, produced champions in the cause of enlightenment, and that with time their voices grew in number.

In this connection, Professor Ramsay Muir, in his history of the town, tells a story worth remembering. George Cooke, in his day a celebrated actor, was once hissed for appearing drunk on the boards of a Liverpool theatre. He pulled himself together, and said venomously 'that he had not come to be insulted by a pack of men every brick in whose detestable town was cemented by the blood of a negro'. Muir adds: 'it speaks strongly, not only for the magnanimity of his audience, but also for the change that was coming over their opinions, that he should have been cheered for his bitter defiance'.

The slave trade, as known to Europe in Wilberforce's time, had had an extended history. As early as the reign of Elizabeth the First, the Hawkins family of Plymouth, together with many others, had engaged in it; and traffic in the human commodity between Africa, and what was known as the Spanish Main, was a principal means of securing to this country a share in the wealth of the New World, in those lands and seas which were for long, and by Papal edict, a monopoly of Portugal and Spain.

When the Spaniards first settled in the Caribbean, their chief need was cheap labour with which to exploit their annexations. They soon found that the native Carib preferred death to working under the conditions of the Spanish plantations. Settlers were therefore forced to look elsewhere, and a solution was soon found in the more docile Negro. Las Casas, a Jesuit writer, appalled by the sufferings of the unwilling Caribs, suggested the importation of Africans. They, so he said, were the sons of Ham, condemned by God to atone in eternal servitude for the sin of their ancestor at the time of the Flood.

However bizarre the theory, particularly as coming from a religious source, it was a practical solution to an increasing difficulty, and it was accepted with enthusiasm. The Caribs continued to die off: meanwhile, the plantations could be worked by importations from another Continent. Before the end of the seventeenth century, the English, the French and the Dutch had all established stations on the coast of West Africa from which slaves could be shipped to the developing West. The workings of demand and supply were as inexorable at that time as at any other.

Until the reign of Queen Anne, the English trade, established as it was, remained unofficial. Negroes apart, the English had long become accustomed to transportation, which was in effect white slavery. Prisoners, such as many of those on the losing side after—

for instance—the Monmouth Rebellion of 1685, were sentenced to forced labour in the West Indies, and the idea was not then new. It was a fact so generally accepted that, in the popular *Beggar's Opera*, fair Polly was made to sing:

> *Were I sold on Indian soil,*
> *Soon as the burning Day was clos'd*
> *I could mock the sultry Toil*
> *When on my Charmer's breast repos'd.*

No one in Gay's early Georgian audience had the slightest difficulty in understanding that Polly meant those words.

Open recognition of the Negro slave trade had come about as early as 1713. One of the provisions of the Peace of Utrecht, which ended the War of the Spanish Succession, was that Great Britain was given the right of importing some 4,800 Negroes into Spanish America within the next thirty years. This was the Asiento Treaty, and by virtue of Britain's strength at sea it gave her what amounted to the principal agency in supply. 'The acquirement of a monopoly in the slave trade was approved by all parties', says G. M. Trevelyan, 'as a sound piece of mercantile policy.' It proved to be so, and if one thing is more certain than another it is that no Spanish official troubled to tot up the number of slaves imported, so long as the market was profitable.

For many years the chief beneficiaries were shipowners in London and Bristol. Liverpool entered the field later. By 1730 Bristol was in the lead, and in that year, when the trade was first thrown open to all comers, Liverpool sent fifteen ships to Africa. She never looked back, except under duress of war. By 1737 her slaver-tonnage had more than doubled: by mid-century, London and even Bristol were behind. There was indeed no check until the War of American Independence, when the traffic was interrupted by privateers. Conditions remained difficult until the conflict was settled.

In the decade 1783–93, slaving boomed. During those years, Liverpool ships made nearly nine hundred round trips. They disposed of 303,737 slaves, who were sold for £15,186,850. By the opening of the War with Revolutionary France Liverpool had acquired well over half the British trade, and nearly half that of all Europe. Although war once again diminished the flow, it did not cease, and in the very last year for which statistics are available—1806-7—one hundred and eighty-five ships carried 43,755 slaves to the plantations. It was indeed a vested interest into which the Abolitionists thrust their swords.

The trade in slaves was not the whole story. Ships loaded at Liverpool with cheap Manchester goods, muskets of an antiquated pattern, gunpowder, beads and fiery spirits. Tawdry goods pleased the simple tastes of the African slave factors: muskets, gunpowder and spirits enabled them to pursue their violent calling. Having crammed their ships with shackled victims for what was known as the Middle Passage, masters disgorged and sold the surviving Negroes on the other side of the Atlantic. Holds were then cleansed of filth which defied description.

The first big profit made, another followed. The same holds which had contained the slaves, and sometimes others still deeper in the ships, were filled with sugar, tobacco, rum and cotton. The vessels thereupon sailed for Liverpool, the owners assured of a further return on their money.

Not only did all classes in the slaving ports have at least some share in the profits, but the African trade had this advantage. No squeamish folk in England ever saw the conditions under which the slaves were bought, transported and resold. All that was visible to them were the goods they had helped to make, which were put into the holds at Liverpool, and the tropical produce with which the vessels returned. It demanded the eye of imagination, and the skilled propagandist, to drive home the iniquity by which a large slice of prosperity arose. It was only the seamen of the slavers who knew the real conditions under which the trade was conducted. They, for the most part, had grown up in a tradition in which humanitarianism played no part; their own terms of service were not idyllic.

Wilberforce himself never sailed in a slaver; never saw at first hand the horror of the African depots. His crusade was based on imaginative sympathy. If his struggle was a long one, if opposition was stubborn and protracted as well as cunning, the adage 'out of sight, out of mind' has to be remembered, for it is certain that, had the facts of the Slave Trade been brought home to the English people visually, the battle for wide support of Abolition would have been won almost as soon as it opened.

2 WILLIAM PITT
From a painting by Thomas Gainsborough

3   WILBERFORCE'S BIRTHPLACE AT HULL, NOW A MUSEUM

III

William Wilberforce, an only son, was born on 24 August 1759 in a substantial Elizabethan house which survives as a museum. He arrived to the sound of victories—the sea battles of Lagos and Quiberon Bay; the land battle of Minden, and the taking of Quebec. They were the triumphs of the war policy of the great Earl of Chatham, whose ablest son, William Pitt, was born in the same year. They raised Britain to eminence in Europe, and to assured status as a colonial Power. Whatever her future, it was certain that, henceforward, her problems and responsibilities would not merely be domestic. At the time only a few rare spirits, among whom were Quakers, saw in the distant traffic an outrage against humanity: when their voice was uplifted, it was soon silenced. The age of the Common Man was far in the future. The Rights of Man, of which so much would be heard later in the century, were still mainly academic. Africa was far away.

Wilberforce's circumstances, which were easy, were soon at odds with his temperament, which, though gay on the surface, was fundamentally serious. His father, Robert Wilberforce, was a partner in a successful business. His mother, who was of the Oxfordshire family of Bird, enjoyed society. He was the third of four children, of whom, beside himself, only one sister reached maturity.

The Wilberforces had long been settled in Yorkshire. The family, originally Wilberfoss, a name deriving from a township eight miles east of York, was prominent at Beverley in the sixteenth century, and had provided a mayor by the time of the outbreak of the Civil War. The same office was filled twice at Hull, in the eighteenth century, by William Wilberforce, the Abolitionist's grandfather. Robert Wilberforce, young William's father, did not live long, and as a child William's own chances of survival did not seem good. He was small, frail, and had weak sight. In later life he expressed thankfulness that he had not been born 'in less civilised times, when it would have been thought impossible to rear so delicate a child'.

If his body was slight, William's mind was vigorous, and his temper affectionate. At seven, he was sent to the local grammar school, which had already produced, in Andrew Marvell, a

Parliamentary notable and an admired poet. William soon made his mark. 'Even then his elocution was so remarkable', wrote Isaac Milner, later Dean of Carlisle and a large influence in his life, 'that we used to set him upon a table and make him read aloud as an example to the other boys.'

Robert Wilberforce died when his son and heir was nine years old. His mother then sent him to an uncle who had houses at Wimbledon and in St. James's Place. He went to a school at Putney, where, so he said later, 'they taught everything and nothing'.

William found the Wimbledon household congenial. His aunt was religious, an admirer of the preacher George Whitefield, exponent of Methodism. In their biography of their father Robert and Samuel Wilberforce say: 'the lively affections of his heart, warmed by the kindness of his friends, readily assumed their tone; and one at least who then met him remarked in him a rare and pleasing character of piety in his twelfth year'.

Such precocious leanings were not to the taste of his mother. She travelled south, to remove him from what she considered to be unfortunate influences. 'I deeply felt the parting', said William, who had become devoted to his uncle and aunt: 'I loved them as parents: indeed I was almost broken-hearted at the separation.' He returned to Hull, and it became the object of his family and friends 'to charm away that serious spirit which had taken possession of his youthful bosom'.

The habits of society in the Hull of that day forwarded the design. 'It was as gay a place as could be found out of London', so William recorded:

> The theatre, balls, great suppers and card parties were the delight of the principal families of the town. This mode of life was at first distressing to me, but by degrees I acquired a relish for it, and became as thoughtless as the rest. I was everywhere invited and caressed. The religious impressions which I had gained at Wimbledon continued for a considerable time after my return to Hull, but my friends spared no pains to stifle them. I might almost say that no pious parent ever laboured more to impress a beloved child with sentiments of piety, than they did to give me a taste for the world and its diversions.

Always an apt pupil, William fell in with his friends' way of life, and an uncommon skill in singing, which he soon discovered,

made him still more popular. Education of a mild sort was continued
at the Grammar School of Pocklington, where the master, 'a man
of easy and polished manners, and an elegant scholar' commended
himself to the family. This master had formerly been a Fellow of
St. John's College, Cambridge, and it was at his advice that William
went to the University at the age of seventeen. By that time, he had
at least one literary composition to his credit. At the age of fourteen,
so it is said, he had been moved to indite a letter to the editor of the
Yorkshire Gazette. Its subject had been condemnation of slavery.

IV

Lady Margaret Beaufort's foundation of St. John's had already
nurtured Wyatt, Ascham, Burghley, Strafford, Fairfax and Stilling-
fleet; it was later to harbour Wordsworth. It has always honoured
Wilberforce, and it contains a characteristic portrait; but to a youth
in affluent circumstances it then offered little but distraction.
William's tutor encouraged him to work as little as had his mother.
By the deaths of his grandfather, father and an uncle, he had been
left master of an independent fortune, which was under his mother's
sole guardianship. He was already assured that he could do what he
liked, and that even a life of dissipation was unlikely to be frowned
upon.

His entry into Cambridge society was not propitious:

> I was introduced, on the very first night of my arrival, to as licentious
> a set of men as can well be conceived. They drank hard, and their
> conversation was even worse than their lives. I lived amongst them for
> some time, though I never relished their society—often indeed I was
> horror-struck at their conduct—and after the first year I shook off in a
> great measure my connection with them

William soon found more congenial spirits 'There was no one at all
like him for powers of entertainment', wrote Thomas Gisborne, a
contemporary. 'Always fond of repartee and discussion, he seemed
entirely free from conceit and vanity.' He added that:

> There was always a great Yorkshire pie in his rooms, and all were
> welcome to partake of it. My rooms and his were back to back, and

often when I was raking out my fire at ten o'clock, I heard his melodious voice calling aloud to me to come and sit with him before I went to bed. It was a dangerous thing to do, for his amusing conversation was sure to keep me up so late, that I was behind-hand the next morning.

Gisborne was an undergraduate who needed to work. Wilberforce, who had no such stimulus, increasingly found himself spending time with Fellows of the College.

But [he wrote] those with whom I was intimate did not act towards me the part of Christians, or even of honest men. Their object seemed to be, to make and keep me idle. If ever I appeared studious, they would say to me: 'Why in the world should a man of your fortune trouble yourself with fagging?' I was a good classic, and acquitted myself well in the college examinations; but mathematics, which my mind greatly needed, I almost entirely neglected, and was told I was too clever to require them. Whilst my companions were reading hard and attending lectures, card parties and idle amusements consumed my time. The tutors would often say within my hearing, that '*they* were mere saps, but that I did all by talent'. This was poison to a mind constituted like mine.

Wilberforce wronged himself. While the lazy, stupid and sycophantic attitude of the dons might indeed have imbued a less virile character than his with an erroneous sense of his powers, the observant Gisborne was right when he said that William was free from vanity. That being so, he was not deceived by flattery, and if he did no work at Cambridge, at least he did not comfort himself by thinking that his mind and abilities needed no embellishment.

William did not leave Cambridge before making up his mind about his future. Three possibilities lay open: a life of pleasure; a life of business; or a life in public service. Pleasure, so he had already found, did not satisfy him, though he never scorned it. The merchant and banking house at Hull from which he drew his income had been managed for him during his minority by his cousin, Abel Smith, who was willing to continue the part. William therefore, young as he was, determined that larger affairs would engage him, and that he would stand for the House of Commons.

He was only twenty-one, but the earlier years of the reign of George III were those of youth. The Sovereign himself had succeeded to the throne at the age of twenty-two. His famous minister, William Pitt, would take high office when he was but little older.

Horatio Nelson, born a year before Wilberforce and Pitt, was a post-captain at the age of twenty, and each case showed that assumption of responsibility when scarcely fledged could lead to a brilliant future.

Pitt and Wilberforce had met at Cambridge, though their acquaintanceship had been slight, Pitt being of another temper. He had been at Pembroke, 'a sober, staid college, and nothing but solid study there'. At Pembroke, instead of cards and the fun of sharing Yorkshire pies, Pitt immersed himself in Greek and Roman literature; in astronomy; mathematics; Shakespeare and civil law. He was equipping himself to follow his father's career as a Parliamentarian, training towards an arduous political life, which would tax every particle of his endurance.

V

Friendship between Wilberforce and Pitt came about in London. Early in 1780, Wilberforce had made a preliminary canvass of some three hundred freemen of Hull who earned their living by Thames-side. He lodged in the Adelphi. He and Pitt, who was about to be called to the Bar, met in the Gallery of the House of Commons, where they listened to debates on the disastrous course of the American War.

Differing widely in temperament as in circumstances, Wilberforce volatile, emotional, laughter-loving, socially at ease, Pitt intellectual, cool and reserved, they were united in opposition to the Government of the day; and in moments of relaxation discussed the world's affairs at the premises of a certain Mr. Goosetree, in Pall Mall, forming part of 'a Society of young Ministers [as an unkind observer once called it, with unintending prophecy] who are to fight under Pitt's banner'.

Wilberforce returned to Hull in the autumn of 1780 to celebrate his coming of age, and to prepare for the excitements of his first Parliamentary election. Despite the opposition of the weighty 'interest' of Lord Rockingham, of Sir George Savile and of the King's Government, the result was almost a foregone conclusion. Wilberforce belonged to Hull, as had his family before him; he was personally liked: although so young, he could already speak fluently and with conviction; he had taken trouble with his canvass; and he was willing to spend between eight and nine thousand pounds on expenses which were then inevitable in a contest in such a place. He received 1,126 votes. His two opponents polled exactly that number between them.

During the same election, Pitt stood for Cambridge University, but was defeated. Before the year ended, Sir James Lowther made him a present of the borough of Appleby. Lowther believed that the young man was of the same political quality as his father, in which judgment he was right. It was thus that, by January 1781, friendship which had begun in the Gallery was continued on the Floor of the House of Commons. The two young men already knew their destiny.

Pitt was soon in the lead. Within a few weeks he had made a maiden speech on financial reform which was praised by Burke and North, and which led Charles James Fox to put up the orator for Brooks's. 'I doubt not', wrote Wilberforce soon afterwards, 'that I shall, one day or another, see him the first man in the country.'

In June, Pitt delivered a violent attack on the American War, in the spirit of his father, and in December another. Six months later, at the age of twenty-three, he was made Chancellor of the Exchequer in Lord Shelburne's administration. His elevation, though astonishing, came about partly through Shelburne's earlier admiration for Chatham, partly because he was an advocate of peace and—like Pitt—of Free Trade. Although a good speaker, Shelburne was incapable of inspiring confidence, and was therefore a bad leader. George III spoke of him as 'the Jesuit' and even Pitt, who owed him such a splendid start, declared that: 'Whatever sins he might commit as a Minister, he had atoned for them beforehand by serving for nearly a year under Lord Shelburne.' This indeed was the voice of realism, not of gratitude.

For all his talents and popularity, Wilberforce could never hope to keep pace with such a meteor as Pitt. His own maiden speech, delivered on 17 May 1781, was a brief attack on the revenue laws; his second an essay in criticism of the Government's failure to increase the Navy; it included a note on Hull's capacity for building ships. Then, in the year following, he let himself go. Speaking on a motion for putting an end to the war, he told the Ministers that they were more like lunatics than statesmen, and that they had conducted the war itself in 'a cruel, bloody and impractical manner'. When the Ministry of Lord North at last collapsed, and Rockingham was for a time in office, rumours were so strong that Wilberforce was shortly to be included in the Government, with a seat in the Lords, that tradesmen actually solicited his custom for the supply of peers' robes. But Rockingham came and went: Shelburne—having ended the American War—contented himself with giving office to Pitt, and when he resigned, and the King was forced to accept a coalition which included North, Fox and Portland, Pitt was excluded. This was a chance for Wilberforce to make a name for himself in opposition. He soon showed himself dangerous in attack, too clever and too eloquent to be snubbed or ridiculed.

The state of affairs in the Commons gave the friends time for a brief excursion to France, which they enjoyed hilariously. They went to Rheims, to Paris and to Fontainebleau, Marie Antoinette bewitching Wilberforce with her 'engaging manner and appearance', Louis XVI striking him as 'a clumsy, strange figure in immense boots . . . worth going a hundred miles for a sight of him a boar-hunting'. But the stay was cut short by a summons from London. George III, restive under the Coalition he detested, sent for Pitt as a way out of his dilemma.

In December 1783, at the age of twenty-four, Pitt became Prime Minister, in the face of a hostile House of Commons. It was an unprecedented situation. The news was at first received with dis-belief, even with laughter. Pitt had, in fact, much difficulty in forming an administration, and he was the only member of the House of Commons in his own Cabinet. But the King was behind him, and so was the House of Lords. He wisely refused to recommend a dissolution until he felt sure that the country was also on his side, putting his own powers to the test in carrying on the Government in spite of formidable attacks, repeated defeats in the lobbies, and much personal abuse. His confidence that his countrymen would value a fighter was soon to be justified; meanwhile, he had the eloquence and the unwavering support of Wilberforce in the Chamber of the House, though Pitt's obligations to others prevented him from offering his friend a Ministerial post. It was, in fact, a curiosity in Wilberforce's career that never, throughout his years in Parliament, did he once enjoy office. Pitt knew that he could rely on his counsel and support without the bribe of power. Had he insisted, then or later, a little pressure must have brought him almost any post for which he had asked. As it was, when it came to be his turn to press a claim upon Pitt's attention and skill, it was on behalf of a cause which involved others, not himself. It could not have been long before Pitt must have begun to reflect how much easier life would have run, had Wilberforce's character been attended with the usual eagerness for personal prestige, instead of with zeal for a remote object, and if he had not been so insistent on his right to think and vote as an independent Member.

VI

On 24 March 1784, Parliament was dissolved, and Pitt had the chance to prove that he had the support of the country at large in his bid to put it on its feet again, after the humiliation of the American War. The day after the event, but before the news had reached the north, there was a great public meeting in the Castle Yard at York, to debate the nation's affairs. It was bleak and blustery, the oratory was indifferent, but so engrossed were the electors in attention to business that it was several hours before they became impatient at the verbiage.

Tired listeners were refreshed when the Member for Hull clambered upon the speaker's table. His beautiful well-pitched voice reached to the fringes of the audience. 'He spoke like an angel' said one who was present, and although the speech itself lasted more than an hour, no one grumbled. James Boswell was also there. He used a metaphor more homely, though quite as effective. 'I saw what seemed a mere shrimp mount upon the table', he reported: 'but as I listened, he grew, and grew, until the shrimp became a whale.'

In the course of the speech, a messenger brought Wilberforce a note giving him word that Pitt was about to appeal to the people. It was in the Prime Minister's own hand, and it enjoined him to 'take care to keep all our friends together, and *to tear the enemy to pieces*'.

Far from being disconcerted by the interruption, Wilberforce turned it to account, gave his hearers news hot from Westminster, and ended in a burst of applause. He had won the hearts of the Yorkshire freeholders. 'We'll have this little man for our county member', they shouted. Sure enough, Wilberforce and his colleague Duncombe got such a vast majority at the show of hands before the election that rivals accepted defeat without asking for a poll. The price of victory was less than £5,000. 'I can never enough congratulate you on such glorious success', wrote Pitt. It was part of the landslide in Pitt's favour with which voters rewarded youth and pluck. They were tired of the old men. They were glad to try the new.

Although, as one of the Members for the largest county in England, Wilberforce was an important figure in the House of Commons, yet for some time the old zest seemed to have vanished from Parliamentary affairs. Fighting beside Pitt at bay had been bracing: Pitt triumphant was another matter, though there was one cause—reform of the Parliamentary franchise—into which Wilberforce could put enthusiasm. This was a measure dear to the heart of Christopher Wyvill, a fellow-Yorkshireman who gave nearly as long a span to its furtherance as Wilberforce devoted to the slaves. Wyvill had the support of Pitt and Wilberforce, but the motion was defeated, and it was almost half a century before Wyvill's ideas were realised, long after he himself was dead. Equally fruitless was Pitt's effort to bring about free trade between England and Ireland. This was a measure over which Wilberforce was prepared to differ from his constituents, who wished the Government to preserve the protective measures they had enjoyed.

Meanwhile, there was much to beguile a man of means and consequence. London hostesses welcomed him as eagerly as had those of Hull. 'The Prince says he will come at any time to hear you sing', wrote the Duchess of Devonshire after a *soirée* at which the young Member first met the Prince of Wales. He could, and did, mimic excellently, until he was warned by Lord Camden that it was a dangerous habit for a politician. He played faro at Brooks's, and the first day he went there he won twenty-four guineas from the

Duke of Norfolk. But one incident at the gaming table gave him
pause, and also showed his kindness of heart. A friend, who never
played himself, challenged him to take the bank. Wilberforce did
so, and at the end of the session found he had won £600: he also
discovered that among those who had lost most heavily were those
who had not yet inherited their fortunes, and could not easily afford
to pay. He gave them every consideration, but never took the bank
again.

Yet another personal advantage was that as by the death of his
uncle he had inherited Lauriston House, Wimbledon, Wilberforce
was possessed of a comfortable place within easy distance of London,
with enough bedrooms to entertain eight or nine guests. Every day,
while Parliament was sitting, he rode or drove to Westminster,
unless he slept at Henry Bankes's house in town. His life was a whirl.
Typical entries in his diary for the year 1784 run as follows:

Jan. 29.   Windy. House — dined White's by way of forming a Club
           — then Play and supp'd Goosetree's.
Feb. 21.   Continued thaw — dined Lord Camden's. Prince of Wales's
           Levée — Opera — supped Goosetree's — took off [i.e.
           mimicked] people — Bed 3.
Feb. 22.   (Sunday) Very much fatigued — church — dined G.
           Hardinge's, Mrs. Siddons sang charmingly.
Feb. 24.   Very tired — walked — dined Mr. Smith's — then Lady
           Howe's ball, danced till ½ past 4.
Mar. 7.   (Sunday) Morning; church — dined Lord Salisbury's. Then
           with Dundas to Mr. Seaton's to sup with Mrs. Siddons —
           Sir C. and Lady Dorothy. Bed ½ past 2.
Aug. 5.   Dined Pitt's — jolly large party — at night returned to
           Wimbledon. Bed ½ past 4.

It was a taxing round, but he enjoyed it, food included, since he
sometimes noted duck, asparagus, turtle, venison and other delicacies.
He paid for it in strain, in occasional illnesses, and also with his eyes,
so that his lines sometimes ran into one another. But he was avid
for experience, and when Parliament rose he could escape, to the
Lakes, to Brighton, to Teignmouth, to Cambridge. Often he
would take with him a box of books. Although his means enabled
him to do so, he never acquired a country place in the fuller sense
of the term, an establishment he could improve, beautify and make
a settled anchorage. This was sad in one who loved nature and

flowers beyond the common measure—and yet it was characteristic, for Wilberforce, like a butterfly, could never settle long in any one place. Years later, he was still flitting, so that a young admirer, who loved him dearly, could say that it seemed 'as unnatural to see a person of Mr. Wilberforce's standing always on the move as it would be to see a little child still'.

But if, bodily, he was restless, it was not so with his affections. Here he was constant—above all towards Pitt. Their tastes were sympathetic, their friends many, and Wilberforce was never happier than when part of a circle of congenial people, joking, boisterous, exchanging repartee—what was then known as *joining*, after a fencing term.

Pitt, for all his reserve, could at times be merry. One evening, the pair joined a party at the Boar's Head in East Cheap to celebrate Shakespeare's memory. 'Many professed wits were present', said Wilberforce, 'but Pitt was the most amusing of the party, and the readiest and most apt in the required allusions.' Unable to afford a suburban villa, Pitt often made use of Lauriston House, and felt the better for a breath of country air. Better—and sometimes hilarious. One morning he got up early and sowed the flower-beds with fragments of an opera-hat which a friend had worn in London the night before. Together, Pitt and Wilberforce indeed 'heard the chimes at midnight', and it was well that they did so. Life stretched gravely before them, and a man is only young once.

VII

Wilberforce had so much enjoyed his trip with Pitt to France, on the eve of his friend's summons to power, that he determined on another, in which plan he was abetted by his mother. In the summer of 1784, after celebrating his twenty-fifth birthday in style at York races, he went to Scarborough. There he came upon Isaac Milner, who as an usher at Hull Grammar School had so much admired his youthful promise. Wilberforce invited Milner to join the party, and Milner accepted. What his mother said about the arrangement is not recorded.

Milner, although only nine years older than Wilberforce, had already had an astonishing career, and it continued so to be. Large in stature ('the most enormous man it was ever my fate to see in a drawing-room' said a Wilberforce relation), loud in voice, coarse and forthright in expression, brilliantly gifted, Milner was living proof that if a man had talent enough, even poverty in the age of privilege could not keep him down. 'He used to say all he thought, and ask for all he wanted', said one who knew him well, and Milner usually got his way. He had begun to earn his living at a weaver's loom. A sizarship at Cambridge gave him scope for his genius in mathematics, though the status itself involved menial duties. Milner, reproved one day for upsetting a tureen of soup, said: 'When I get into power I will abolish this nuisance'—and he was as good as his word. In the Tripos of 1774 the examiners placed him first, and wrote the word *incomparabilis* after his name. Two years later, he was elected to Fellowships of Queens' College and of the Royal Society. At the time of the Scarborough meeting, Milner was in orders; he held the living of St. Botolph's Cambridge and the University Chair of Natural Philosophy, his province including scientific experiment. He was, for instance, the first to make nitric acid by oxidising ammonia. Milner was on every count a formidable companion for the gay young man who now proposed to set out for the Riviera, by way of Lyons and Avignon, with himself and his friend in one carriage, his mother, sister and two female cousins in another.

The ladies were deposited at Nice, where they settled down in a villa for the winter. Wilberforce and Milner later returned alone, on roads which were by then snow-clogged, and they beguiled the journey by reading *The Rise and Progress of Religion in the Soul*, which had been published forty years earlier by Philip Doddridge, a Nonconformist minister. This, in Milner's view, was 'one of the best works ever written'. Wilberforce was impressed both by his companion and their reading. A natural inclination towards religion deepened to a degree which amounted to a psychological change.

When the next Parliamentary session was over, Wilberforce set out to bring his family back to England. Milner was again his companion. They met the ladies in July at Genoa, and travelled thence to Geneva and the Bernese Oberland. This time, the Greek New Testament occupied attention, 'the most difficult book in the world', as Dr. Johnson once described it, 'for which the study of a lifetime is required'. Milner and Wilberforce grew so absorbed in their pursuit that Wilberforce was taken to task for the infrequency of his visits to the other carriage. 'By degrees' he wrote long after-wards, 'I imbibed his [Milner's] sentiments, though I must confess with shame that they long remained merely as opinions, assented to by my understanding but not influencing my heart.' The cavalcade returned to England by the Rhine and Spa. This time, slow as his conversion may have seemed to himself, there was no return. This time, his mother would be given no chance to beguile him back to acceptance of easier standards. He was his own master, and he intended to remain so.

Milner, directly or indirectly, led him to seek the advice of John Newton, then Rector of St. Mary Woolnoth in Lombard Street. Newton was one of Whitefield's most celebrated successors in the Evangelical line, author of two favourite hymns: 'How sweet the name of Jesus sounds . . .' and 'Glorious things of Thee are spoken . . .', friend of the gentle poet Cowper, and of Wilberforce's kinsmen, the Thorntons. Newton led Wilberforce to think of the slaves. He did so autobiographically.

Newton was then a man of sixty, an eloquent, popular preacher with a variegated life behind him. While Whitefield had spent his youth as a tapster at the Bell Inn, Gloucester, Newton's had been an education at sea. Son of the master of a merchantman, he had been impressed into the Navy, and had felt the harsh side of its discipline. Then he had drifted into the post of overseer at one of the depots on the Gold Coast where slaves were collected for shipment to America. There he led a degraded life, until he was brought back to England by a friend of his father. His new occupation was as mate of a slaver, and he soon had his own command.

It was during Newton's career in the slave trade that 'conversion' came upon him, but it was characteristic of the outlook of his time that transformation in spiritual life brought with it no repugnance towards his occupation. An instance of a rather similar kind is afforded by Richard Kempenfelt, who later sank with the *Royal George*. One of the most practical officers of the Fleet, he was at this time composing startling religious verse, of a sort which would have appealed to Newton, meanwhile, and simultaneously, hard at work on a system of battle-tactics.

Newton's own ship was well conducted, his humanity became proverbial, but it was ill-health, together with a conviction that God had a better use for his talents, not aversion from his way of life, that led him to look for employment ashore. First he became surveyor of tides at Liverpool. Then he sought deacon's orders in the Church of England. His earlier life, and his addiction to Methodism at first caused difficulty, in spite of the fact that he had taught himself the elements of Greek, Latin and Hebrew. But he was received at last within the fold of the Establishment, and from then until his death, at a great age, 'the old African blasphemer' as he described himself, continued to recall with ruthless candour and in lurid terms the pit from which his Creator had lifted him. 'Very unhappy' Wilberforce noted: 'called at Newton's, and bitterly moved: comforted me.' The man who could scourge penitents also knew how to console them.

If 'gravity' should be the business of life, so Wilberforce told his sister, 'gaiety' should be its relaxation: 'but', he added, 'I will give it a more worthy epithet than gay. Let me call it serenity, tranquillity, composure which is not to be destroyed.' Such equipment was formidable. The fashionables among whom Wilberforce continued to live in London distrusted, disliked and above all were bored by 'enthusiasm' in religion, which they considered pertained to the lower orders. But a man who could retain his outward ease, his spontaneity and charm, who did not force his convictions too pressingly upon his friends, remained acceptable, even valued. Yet, things were changed. Wilberforce removed his name from his clubs; and the word 'foining' dropped from his private vocabulary.

Typical of a new sort of friend was Hannah More, whom Wilberforce met at Bath. Her works are no longer read, but in her day she was many-sided and influential. A favourite with Johnson, Reynolds, Burke and Garrick, she had much success as a dramatist, her tragedy, *Percy*, selling four thousand copies in a fortnight. Suddenly, she began to break away from her old life, and she came to regard the theatre as so evil that she even refused to be present when *Percy* was revived, with Mrs. Siddons as heroine. Finally, she withdrew from London altogether, devoting herself to education, and to the composition of works with such titles as *Thoughts on the Importance of the Manners of the Great to General Society*. Of Wilberforce she said: 'That young gentleman's character is one of the most extraordinary I ever knew for talents, virtue and piety', and when Wilberforce heard of Hannah More's decision to give her time and resources to the education of the poor in Somerset, he was moved to say: 'This is truly magnificent, the really sublime in character.'

Where there were such examples, he was eager to follow. In the course of time he closed his Wimbledon house as being the cause of needless expense; gave money to Hannah's schemes; to Yorkshire charities; to friends in difficult circumstances, even encroaching on his capital to do so. And always, the charity was anonymous. 'By management', he concluded, he should be able to give away 'at least one fourth' of his income to the poor.

Grave Wilberforce might have become, and in his diary self-reproachful: but he banished himself only briefly from general society, and never allowed himself to become a prig. In the case of a man who had received so serious a call, this was an achievement for which many must have blessed him, not least the recipients of his gifts.

VIII

On 24 November 1785, Wilberforce noted in his diary: 'Heard the Bible read two hours—Pascal one and a quarter—business the same. Pitt called, and commended Butler's *Analogy*—resolved to write to him, and discover to him what I am occupied about.' Pitt, in hitting upon Butler, had given him the chance he wanted, and in his letter he told his friend of his deepened feelings, adding that it was his intention to withdraw for a time from public life. He said that he would 'ever feel a strong affection' for Pitt, and that he saw no likelihood that they would differ seriously in politics. However, he added, he did not think it likely he could be 'so much of a party man' as he had been hitherto. He went on to say that he dreaded argument over matters which he felt could not be argued, and even suggested that, when next they met, the subject of his letter should not be mentioned.

The reply, sent by the Prime Minister from Downing Street on 2 December, can have left Wilberforce in no doubt whatever how much his friendship meant to Pitt. On receiving Wilberforce's letter, Pitt swept aside the piles of official papers by which he was surrounded, determined to assure him at once of the warmth of his sympathy. It was the act of a man whose human values were right; a man of feeling; a loyal spirit.

> As to any public conduct which your opinions may ever lead you to [wrote Pitt], I will not disguise to you that few things could go nearer my heart than to find myself differing from you essentially on any great principle. I trust and believe that it is a circumstance which can hardly occur. But if it ever should, and even if I should experience as much pain in such an event, as I have hitherto encouragement and pleasure in the reverse, believe me it is impossible that it should shake the sentiments of affection and friendship which I bear towards you, and which I must be forgetful and insensible indeed if I ever could part with. They are sentiments engraved on my heart, and will never be effaced or weakened. . . .

Seizing on Wilberforce's idea that 'the character of religion is not a gloomy one, and that it is not that of an enthusiast', Pitt hoped that his friend's intention of withdrawal would not lead him to 'melancholy or superstition' and that, if it furthered meditation, this might later result in action. He could not think of Wilberforce as a contemplative.

Dismissing the idea that the pair of them should not discuss such an important change in Wilberforce's outlook, Pitt asked, as a 'mark both of your friendship and of the candour that belongs to your mind', that Wilberforce would open himself 'fully and without reserve to one, who, believe me, does not know how to separate your happiness from his own'. Tomorrow, said Pitt, was not too soon. 'I am going into Kent,' he said, 'and can take Wimbledon in my way. Reflect, I beg of you, that no principles are the worse for being discussed. . . .'

With such a letter in his hand, signed 'affectionately and unalterably yours', by the first Commoner in England, there could be only one answer. 'Much affected by it', Wilberforce noted, and of course agreed to meet. There was a two-hour discussion the very next day. 'I admitted that as far as I could conform to the world, with a perfect regard to my duty to God, myself and my fellow creatures, I was bound to do it', said Wilberforce, adding 'that no inward feelings ought to be taken as demonstrations of the Spirit being in any man, but only the change of disposition and conduct'.

Pitt tried to reason Wilberforce out of his convictions, but 'found himself unable to contest their correctness, if Christianity were true'. The talk turned to Bishop Butler, whose *Analogy* Pitt had praised. His was a book which, without much grace of style, depends for its effect upon the force of its reasoning, one which, a century later, was to attract, in Gladstone, another Prime Minister. But even in Butler's case, so Pitt declared, his 'work raised in his mind more doubts than it had answered'. 'The fact was,' recorded Wilberforce, 'he was so absorbed in politics that he had never given himself time for due reflection on religion.'

On spiritual matters the two agreed to differ. But by Pitt's persuasion, the old familiar intercourse was resumed within a very few months. 'Pitt's before House—dined.' 'Dined Pitt's and sat with him.' 'Went to Holwood with Pitt.' 'Hurried to House, no business, Pitt having got the gout—saw him.' The private diary soon began to fill up with entries characteristic of earlier days. 'They were exactly like brothers', said one who often saw them together at this time. Nevertheless, there was a change in their relationship. Pitt had to manage a Party, as well as to govern the country. He would no longer enjoin his friend, as he had in the note to York, to 'tear the enemy to pieces'. In the affairs of the House of Commons he would rely increasingly on another, Henry Dundas, for counsel in the more mundane problems. Such a turn was inevitable, and it implied an even greater respect for each other on the part of the two men: Wilberforce for Pitt's unshakeable patriotism and Parliamentary management: Pitt for Wilberforce's integrity and charity of outlook. Politics, even at their best, are a dusty business, an affair of compromise, of bribery by power and concession, of twists and tedium. If Pitt would never again allow himself to play the fool in Wilberforce's company, he could still rely on finding in his friend a proportioned outlook and an inner tranquillity; moreover, if Wilberforce was at times inclined to force conversation into channels where Pitt did not care to follow, he was never in danger of becoming a bore.

It was, in fact, with serenity that the year closed—in the 'composure and happiness of a true Christian'. Wilberforce was even able to assure his mother, anxious as ever for his temporal well-being, that he did not mean to become a recluse:

> This would merit no better name than desertion, and if I were thus to fly from the part where Providence has placed me, I know not how I could look for the blessing of God upon my retirement; and without this heavenly assistance, either in the world or in solitude, our own endeavours will be equally ineffectual.

IX

Peace, frugality, freer trade: these were the principles upheld by Pitt in the years which gave Great Britain an essential breathing-space between defeat in the American War and the protracted struggle with France which was to absorb her energies increasingly during the last decade of the eighteenth century. There were other large issues which engaged public men: the question of responsibility for the future of India, which gave occasion for Burke, with golden eloquence, to enunciate the idea of trusteeship; the long-drawn-out impeachment of Warren Hastings: Catholic Emancipation, with which was linked the question of how Ireland should be governed. On these matters, Pitt could command Wilberforce's vote and sometimes his eloquence, but Wilberforce's main interests lay elsewhere. He met one success, and one reverse, in his immediate activities. He tried to carry an amending Bill softening some of the savagery of the existing penal laws, the most striking provision being the substitution of hanging for burning as the capital punishment for women convicted of murdering their husbands. The Commons were favourable, but the Bill was defeated in the Lords, ostensibly on points of law, actually through the persuasion of Lord Loughborough, who did not see eye to eye with Pitt's Law officers.

Rejection led Wilberforce to consider the whole question of the effectiveness of punishment as a deterrent to crime.

> The barbarous custom of hanging [he wrote to Wyvill] has been tried too long, and with the success which might have been expected of it. The most effectual way of preventing the greater crimes is by punishing the smaller, and by endeavouring to suppress that general spirit of licentiousness which is the parent of every species of vice.

The reasoning was uncertain, for it was rather by preventing than by punishing the 'smaller crimes' that improvement would result. As for 'licentiousness', this was in part a reaction against what, for so many, were the hard conditions under which they lived: conditions quite unknown to men of fortune.

A reading of Dr. Joseph Woodward's *History of the Society for the Reformation of Manners in the Year 1692* gave Wilberforce the idea of founding a similar society to combat what he conceived to be the loose standards of the day. He had no difficulty in enlisting support. No party issues were involved: no legitimate vested interests. The Archbishop of Canterbury blessed it; he found a blameless duke to officiate as the first President; Lord North lent his name; Pitt approved, and when, in the fullness of time, the King was approached, the objects so appealed to George III's piety that on 1 June 1787 he issued a Royal Proclamation against Vice and Immorality, the society becoming known as the Proclamation Society. When, in 1802, its place was taken by the better-known Society for the Suppression of Vice, it came to be the butt of Sydney Smith's mordant humour. 'A corporation of informers', he called it, 'supported by large contributions, bent on suppressing not the vices of the rich but the pleasures of the poor', and on reducing their life 'to its regular standard of decorous gloom' while 'the gambling houses of St. James's remain untouched'. Such impeccable associations were not difficult to form, but their effect was not marked, and they served to recall an unpopular period in English history, the reign of the Puritans. It was therefore fortunate that Wilberforce's energies soon found a task which would require sustained effort and the employment of all his powers, instead of one which was, in any case, the concern of innumerable preachers of all denominations, part of their professional business.

It was in the year 1787, when Wilberforce was still under thirty, that influences seemed to converge and concentrate on the matter of the Slave Trade. It had already been the subject of a literature stretching back more than a century, which had been mainly one of attack. Advocates rested their case on necessity, on custom, and on the fact that the 'West Indian interest' was powerful both in the City and in Parliament. At one time, the law had also been on their side.

The Quakers had been the first body to make an organised stand. In 1724 they had passed a resolution condemning slavery and the slave trade together. In 1758, in step with brethren of Pennsylvania, they proceeded to warn, and in 1761 to disown, all Friends who continued to take part in it. The Wesleyans, meanwhile, had followed their lead, Wesley himself entering the lists.

West Indian planters had been accustomed, on their visits to England, to bring with them a number of their domestic slaves, who sometimes ran away. In such cases, when they found a minister to baptise them, and warm-hearted citizens to become their godfathers, they enjoyed some protection against the arbitrary power of their master. Cases were even known where godfathers would threaten masters with a suit at law if they attempted to remove the slaves from England.

In 1729 the West Indian community, exasperated at what could happen to those whom they deemed to be their private property, appealed to the Law officers of the Crown for an opinion. Attorney-General Yorke and Solicitor-General Talbot gave them all they wanted. They stated that neither residence in England nor baptism affected a master's 'right and property' in a slave, and that a master 'may legally compel him to return again to the plantations'. Very soon, announcements of slave-auctions actually appeared in the newspapers. Rewards were offered for runaways. Capturing slaves and putting them safe on board ship became almost a trade in the East End of London. But the law, in carrying matters so far, had begun to create Abolitionists among the public at large. If Britons, as a popular song maintained, never should be slaves, they increasingly disliked the idea of human beings auctioned by their fellow-countrymen.

The first great step towards Abolition was made by Granville Sharp, who, at intervals from work at a clerkship in the Ordnance

Department, took up the cause of the Negroes. After being involved in a personal incident with a runaway slave, whom he managed to protect, Sharp devoted two years to the composition of a book called *The Injustice and Dangerous Tendency of Tolerating Slavery in England.* In this treatise he recalled an earlier opinion given by Chief Justice Holt that every slave entering England became free. He supported his case with a learned exposition of certain principles of Common Law. Legal contradiction, on so vital a subject, was not to be tolerated, and in 1772, Mansfield, the greatest lawyer of his day, fulfilled Sharp's hope that the case of James Somerset, a captured runaway, could be made a test for settling, once and for all, the conflict between Holt's ruling and that of Yorke and Talbot. The case was heard at three sittings, at each of which the Court was crowded. From the first, it was clear that Mansfield, reluctant as he was to deal a blow to property, sympathised with long-established notions of freedom on English soil, and when, on 22 June, he delivered his judgment, he made history. 'Tracing the subject to natural principles,' he said, 'the claim of slavery never can be supported. The power claimed never was in use here or acknowledged by the Law.'

The decision was momentous, and gave an immediate and lasting impetus to the movement for general Abolition of the trade in human beings. Although slavery was to continue on British soil overseas for more than sixty years, from that moment it ceased to be recognised in the home country. With public opinion as it then stood, it was impossible that Mansfield's judgment would be reversed. It is estimated that over fourteen thousand slaves then in England were affected by the ruling, an astonishing number, concentrated mainly in the seaports.

Meanwhile, the Trade itself continued. Mansfield's judgment indirectly led to a Commission of Enquiry into its conditions; but the result was disregarded, and in 1776 the House of Commons rejected the first of a long series of resolutions against it which was moved by Hartley, a predecessor of Wilberforce in the seat for Hull. Some years later, a Bill was introduced to prevent servants of the Crown from engaging in the business of the African Company. This was the occasion for a petition organised by the Quakers opposing the Trade. Lord North's response was a typical example

of the sort of reply which, for many years to come would be evoked
by the subject:

> The object and tendency of the Petition ought to recommend it to
> every humane breast; and it did credit to the feelings of the most mild
> and humane set of Christians in the world. But still he was afraid that
> it would be found impossible, to abolish the Slave Trade . . . for it was
> a trade which had, in some measure, become necessary to almost every
> nation in Europe; and as it would be next to an impossibility to induce
> them all to give it up and renounce it for ever, so he was apprehensive
> that the wishes of the humane petitioners could not be accomplished.

Courtesy, flattery, condemnation in principle, resignation to facts—
such were the obstacles against which Abolitionists would struggle,
when, indeed, they did not meet with an opposition openly
venomous and violent.

The volume of protest soon began to swell. The Quakers formed
a committee of six—William Dillwyn, George Harrison, Samuel
Hoare, Thomas Knowles, John Lloyd and Joseph Woods—who
were permanently engaged in the cause. Granville Sharp continued
to be a tower of strength. The Rev. James Ramsay, who had spent
nineteen years at St. Kitts, returned home, to a living at Teston in
Kent, burning to redress the Negroes' wrongs. Presently there came
an advocate prepared to give his life to benefit the slaves. This was
Thomas Clarkson, who, after a brilliant school career at St. Paul's,
continued his education at Cambridge—by coincidence, at Wilberforce's old college.

Clarkson won a prize for a Latin essay. The subject had been
chosen by Dr. Pickard, Master of Magdalene—*Anne Liceat invitos
in servitutum dare?* 'Is it right to make men slaves against their will?'
Pickard was known for his anti-slavery views, and Clarkson, eager
to distinguish himself, mastered every book on the subject of West
Africa and the West Indian trade that he could find. He soon met
those who could tell him much at first hand, could fire his imagination.
Dillwyn, Sharp and Ramsay opened their hearts to the generous
youth. Soon, he abandoned the clerical career on which he was about
to embark, determined to spend his time in the prosecution of one
object. And so, by the summer of 1787, with the Quakers as a
nucleus, there came into being a formal 'Committee for the
Abolition of the Slave Trade', with Sharp as its first Chairman.

Among their duties it was necessary to find a Parliamentarian who would be their champion.

In 1784 Ramsay had published an *Essay on the Treatment and Conversion of the African Slaves in the Sugar Colonies*, the first of a series of pamphlets on the subject. Among its readers was the author's old friend and patron, Sir Charles Middleton, and his public-spirited wife. Middleton was at the centre of things. He was Comptroller of the Navy, Member of Parliament for Rochester, a friend of Pitt.

Middleton knew and liked Wilberforce, who was invited to Keston. There the enthusiasts had little difficulty in enlisting Wilberforce's help with a subject which was already near to his heart. 'It was just one of those many impulses', he said later, 'which were all giving to my mind the same direction.' 'God Almighty', he wrote in his Journal, 'has set before me two great objects, the suppression of the Slave Trade and the reformation of manners.'

It was Wilberforce's way, when any idea impressed him, to gather evidence about it from every possible source; to converse; to discuss; to listen; to meditate; to prepare memoranda. There could be nothing secret in any matter of general interest which engaged the prolonged attention of a Member for Yorkshire, and Pitt would soon have known how things were going with his friend. It must have been the cause of some anxiety, for championship of Abolition was not a matter to be lightly undertaken by a man who, for all his energy, was sensitive and fragile. Pitt would have reflected that Burke himself had contemplated the task, but had refrained from fear of rousing a storm which would have split his party. Pitt, in a sense, was in the same position as Burke, but he knew that the plea of party unity did not apply to his friend. The task would be painful and exhausting, but it would be worthy of Wilberforce's powers, and would remove the last temptation for him to withdraw from the world of affairs.

It thus came about one day in the summer of 1787 Pitt, Grenville and Wilberforce—three men much of an age, each to leave a mark upon the history of their country—sat together 'at the root of an old tree at Holwood, just above the steep descent into the vale of Keston'. Pitt then asked the question which Wilberforce most wanted to hear. 'Why don't you give notice of a motion on the

subject of the Slave Trade?' he said. Had he not already taken great
pains to collect evidence? Was not the subject admirably suited to
his talents and character? 'Do not lose time', Pitt added, 'or the
ground may be occupied by another.' With Pitt's encouragement,
nothing now stood in the way.

Clarkson provided the occasion for a positive declaration. This
was made at a dinner-party graced by the presence of Sir Joshua
Reynolds, James Boswell, William Windham,[1] Sir Charles
Middleton and Dr. Johnson's friend Bennett Langton. 'What about
the welfare of the West Indies and the prosperity of Liverpool?'
someone ventured. 'Rather let Liverpool and the Islands be swallowed
up by the sea', said another, 'than this monstrous system of iniquity
be carried on.' Langton then asked Wilberforce if he would
champion Abolition in the House. Wilberforce agreed; nor had he
any objection to Clarkson making the matter known to his friends
in the City.

> There was then no example upon record [wrote Wilberforce's sons in
> their filial biography] of any such achievement, and in entering upon
> the struggle it was of the utmost moment that its leader should be one
> who could combine, and so render irresistible, the scattered sympathies
> of all religious classes.

Granville Sharp had no doubt that the Committee had found the
right man:

> Mr. W. is to introduce the business to the House. His position as
> member for the largest county, the great influence of his personal
> connections, added to an amiable and unblemished character, secure
> every advantage to the cause.

[1] Neither Boswell nor Windham were themselves Abolitionists, but it was to
Boswell that Dr. Johnson dictated an argument based on the proposition that 'no
man is by nature the property of another', and it was Boswell who recorded a toast
given at Oxford by Johnson: 'Here's to the next insurrection of the Negroes in the
West Indies.'

2 THE STRUGGLE

No advocate of the Abolition of the Slave Trade could have been under any delusion that the task would be simple. The ill-success of the idea of Parliamentary Reform had shown how massive were the forces opposed to change of any kind. Public opinion was not yet mobilised, and enthusiasts, though they came from varied sides of society, included few of rank or wealth. Although Pitt was among them, and the cause would be sustained by some of the nobler spirits of the age, the influence of the Government as such could not be committed, for Pitt's Cabinet, still drawn from the House of Lords, held many opposed to the measure, including his disloyal Lord Chancellor, Thurlow, who had great influence with the King, and Sydney, who dealt with Colonial affairs. 'One must have gone through as much as I have,' a weary Napoleon once said, 'in order to be acquainted with all the difficulties of doing good.' When that good was distant, when it touched the pockets of those other than the reformers, when it affected the fortunes of no particular political party, difficulties increased. And at the very outset of the campaign, Wilberforce himself fell ill.

Before that misfortune, much had happened. Pitt, through the Ambassador in Paris, had sounded the views of the Government in France, and found strong resistance to any change, at least until Britain herself had given a decisive lead. As for himself, Pitt set about mastering the whole business. 'It would delight you to hear

Pitt talk on this question', Wilberforce told Wyvill. Pitt spoke with Ramsay, with Clarkson and others who could give him knowledge, without which enthusiasm was useless. In January 1788 he wrote to Wilberforce from Holwood: 'If you could contrive to come here tonight or tomorrow, I would stay another day quiet in the country, and should like extremely to have a full prose.'

Others were at stretch. Clarkson set out upon a fact-finding tour. At Bristol he found the subject in everybody's mouth, 'but although everybody seemed to execrate it, no one thought of its Abolition'. He soon proved, from ship's muster-books, the high proportion of deaths among seamen engaged in the Trade. He took measurements of the slave quarters in two ships then in port. He saw in the windows of a Liverpool shop the leg-shackles, hand-cuffs, thumb-screws and mouth-openers for forcible feeding which were used on board, and wisely bought a specimen of each. Local suspicions were quickly aroused, and Clarkson was once in danger of being hustled into the sea as he watched a furious gale from a pier-head. He only escaped after blows had been exchanged.

The opposition were indeed mobilising forces—at Court, in Society, in Parliament. No merely private information could hope to refute evidence about a Trade which its participants stated to be both 'necessary and humane', and which, so it was said, was being attacked by 'mere busy-bodies'. Pitt thereupon decided that a Committee of the Privy Council should make a formal enquiry 'into the conditions of British commercial intercourse with Africa'. Before anyone spoke on the matter in Parliament, evidence must be assembled by an official body.

For Wilberforce, the mounting excitement, the strain of incessant work, proved too much. By the end of March 1788, he collapsed with what appeared to be serious intestinal trouble. 'There's Wilberforce', said a Cambridge acquaintance, pointing to the sufferer. 'He can't last three weeks!' Even the doctors thought the same. 'He has no stamina to last a fortnight', so they told the family, advising the Bath waters as offering the last hope of a cure.

Before he left for the West country, Wilberforce sent for Pitt. Would Pitt, whatever happened, himself move the resolution in Parliament, now that he, Wilberforce, could not do so himself? Pitt's answer came from the heart. Caution, party difficulties, royal

4 THOMAS CLARKSON
From a portrait by
C. F. von Breda

5 ISAAC MILNER
from a portrait by
G. H. Harlow,
hitherto unpublished

6 THE OLD HOUSE OF COMMONS. ADDINGTON IN THE CHAIR. PITT SPEAKING
WILBERFORCE IN FRONT OF THE LAST PILLAR ON THE LEFT

From a painting by K. A. Hickel, 1793

coldness, the possible effect on his own career—all were forgotten. 'With a warmth of principle and friendship', said Wilberforce, 'that has made me love him better than ever I did before,' Pitt gave his promise. He would do everything, if his friend so wished, which Wilberforce would have done himself. Wilberforce was a professed and practising Christian: he found in the sceptical, worldly, practical Pitt, virtues worthy of the cause they had taken up. Such unreserved and generous help was even more than he had a right to look for. Although Wilberforce reached Bath in a grievous physical state, it was with a quiet mind. Pitt had, in fact, put him on the road to recovery.

Medicine helped—in this case, minute doses of opium, a drug which his doctor, Pitcairn, had difficulty in persuading the patient to use. Once the corner was turned, progress was speedy. By 5 May, Wilberforce was able to leave Bath for a visit to Cambridge, where he spent a peaceful month at St. John's living regularly and quietly, seeing much of Isaac Milner, dining in Hall. He completed his cure with a visit to the Lakes, but there, Society caught up with him. 'The tour of the Lakes', so he wrote to Newton, 'has become so fashionable that the banks of the Thames are scarcely more public than those of Windermere. . . . At the moment my cottage over-flows with guests.'

II

The way in which Pitt handled the business in the House of Commons occasioned a tribute to, as well as from, Wilberforce. He superintended the Privy Council enquiry in person. He invited Sharp to Downing Street, where Sharp said that the Committee over which he presided aimed at nothing short of total Abolition of the Trade. Pitt replied that 'his heart was with them, and that he considered himself pledged to Mr. Wilberforce that the cause should not sustain any injury from his indisposition'. But, he added, some delay was inevitable; serious proceedings could not begin until the Privy Council's enquiry was completed. Pitt would move that the House bound itself to consider the circumstances of the Slave Trade early in the next session, and this he accordingly did, on

9 May, soon after Wilberforce had reached Cambridge. Should the principal advocate be still unwell by that time, he himself would introduce the question.

Fox then rose, and said he had meant to move the business himself, but that:

> when he heard that the member for Yorkshire had resolved to take it up, he was unaffectedly rejoiced, not only knowing that gentleman's purity of principles and sincere love for the rights of humanity but because, from a variety of considerations as to the character and situations in which different men stood in that House, there was something that made him honestly think that it was better that the business should be in the hands of the honourable gentleman than in his, and that it would come from him with more might, more authority, and more probability of success than from himself.

He further declared that he thought the Trade should be destroyed, not regulated. So did Burke, committing himself to the 'full, clean course of Abolition'. Pitt—Burke—Fox: when three such men spoke on the same side, the cause must indeed have appeared exceptional.

One other member, Sir James Johnstone, made some pertinent remarks. He pointed to the possible effects on the minds of the slaves themselves of discussion at Westminster. It was, he said, a cogent reason for doing something at once, 'lest the poor creatures' hopes might be raised too high, and bad consequences follow'. He said that he had recently heard from Grenada that they were going about 'in excited hope and faith' saying: 'Mr. Wilberforce for negro, Mr. Fox for negro, the Parliament for negro, God Almighty for negro.'

Opponents of the measure bided their time, but before the session closed they gave tongue—unwisely, as it happened. Old Sir William Dolben, Member for Oxford University, had been moved to go aboard a slave ship lying in the Thames. He had been so appalled by surveying the quarters in which the Negroes were confined in their voyage across the Atlantic that he gave notice of a Bill for limiting the number to be carried in proportion to the tonnage of the ship concerned.

In the debate on the second reading of Dolben's Bill, since the House was discussing a practical measure, not a principle, champions of the Trade were forced into the open. Liverpool merchants were heard by counsel at the Bar of the House, and their representatives were compelled to admit that the average death-rate on the notorious Middle Passage was from five to ten per cent according to the length of voyage and the weather encountered, and that in one case no less than a third of the slaves had died. More accurate figures showed that those estimates were wide of the mark: the average mortality, as Wilberforce could prove, was higher still.

Pitt was so moved by the revelations at the Bar, and so angered by the refusal of the opposition to support regulation of any kind, that he declared:

> If the Trade cannot be carried on in a manner different to that stated by the honourable members opposite to me, I will retract what I said on a former day against going into the general question, and waiving every other discussion than what has this day taken place, I will give my vote for the utter abolition of a Trade which is shocking to humanity, is abominable to be carried on by any country, and reflects the greatest dishonour on the British senate and the British nation. The Trade, as the petitioners propose to carry it on, without any regulation, is contrary to every humane, to every Christian principle, to every sentiment that ought to inspire the breast of man.

The regulating Bill was thereupon carried by the Commons—but there was still the House of Lords, and the House, with such men as Thurlow in it, was not a repository of enlightenment. Thurlow called the measure a 'five days' fit of philanthropy': merchants would be ruined, he said. A few peers supported the Bill, but most followed Thurlow's lead. Lord Heathfield, the defender of Gibraltar, calculated that a Negro in a slave ship had nearly twice as much cubic air to breathe as a British soldier in a tent—an extraordinarily irrelevant tit-bit. The Duke of Chandos thought the passage of any such Bill might lead to a Negro rising and a massacre of the whites; a recurrent and not unreasonable fear. Admiral Lord Rodney, victor of the Battle of the Saintes, which had helped to save the West Indians in the course of the American War, was frankly anxious lest Britain should lose the Trade to the French. He had never heard of a Negro being cruelly treated, he said, in all the time he had been in the area concerned, and he had often expressed a wish that the English labourer might be half as happy.

Peers, however illustrious, could say what they pleased—but

Pitt's back was up. He told Grenville that, if the Bill were defeated in the Lords, he would not remain in the same Cabinet with its opposers. He had his way, but only by two votes.

III

The events of the summer of 1788 had hastened Wilberforce's convalescence. Parliament was committed to a full discussion of the Slave Trade: Pitt had shown himself to detest its cruelties, and had risked the very existence of his Government to ensure immediate regulation. By December, the invalid was restored, had once again settled in London, and was immersed in business with Clarkson, Ramsay and those whom Pitt jocularly called his 'white negroes'. They worked themselves furiously, sometimes to exhaustion.

For his part, Wilberforce was not allowed to concentrate the whole of his attention on the Slave Trade, for the country's political affairs were suddenly in crisis. George III had gone out of his mind. One manifestation of his condition had been stopping his carriage in Windsor Great Park, getting out of it, and addressing an oak tree as the King of Prussia. The Whigs were demanding the assumption of a Regency by the Prince of Wales, whose first act, so it was believed, would be to dismiss Pitt and send for Fox. Pitt, for his part, was determined that, if a Regent should prove necessary, he should be appointed under such conditions as Parliament might desire. Wilberforce stood by his friend, convinced that Pitt was upholding constitutional right, patriotism and honesty in a world of intrigue—and intrigue was the word. Thurlow was actually giving away Cabinet secrets to the Prince at the price of retaining the Woolsack in a new Government, to such infamy can the lust for power lead clever men. Happily the King recovered; the Prince had already been caused to acknowledge the sovereignty of Parliament; and Thurlow, in a mood of solemnity, declared: 'When I forget my debt of gratitude to the King, may God forget me.' Fox's retort to this was: 'It is the very best thing He could do for you'; but Wilkes murmured: 'He'll see you damned first.'

The domestic danger passed, Wilberforce became re-engrossed

in the slavery issue, and his sons, in their biography, describe his study as it was at this time:

> On one chair sat a Yorkshire constituent, manufacturing or agricultural; on another a petitioner for charity or a House of Commons client; on another a Wesleyan preacher; while side by side with an African, a foreign missionary, or a Haytian professor, sat perhaps some man of rank who sought a private interview, and whose name had accidentally escaped announcement.

Hannah More was more pithy. It was, she said, like 'Noah's Ark, full of beasts, clean and unclean'. Among the cleaner sort was James Stephen, barrister and later Master in Chancery. Stephen had lived for some years at St. Kitts, like Ramsay, and had been so repulsed by what he had seen of slavery at close quarters that he had refused, in the face of custom, to own a single slave himself. He was a year older than Wilberforce, and his experience and abilities made him a valuable ally. All the more valued was he since Ramsay, who had been singled out by the more violent of the West Indian planters for a battery of calumny and personal abuse which in its own way was as shameful as the Trade, became broken in health, and was soon dead. One opponent of Abolition, who does not deserve to be nameless though he shall be here, announced the news to his illegitimate son at St. Kitts: 'Ramsay is dead—I have killed him.'

In April 1789 the Privy Council's Report was ready to be examined. The material was marshalled under five heads: (1) On the Civilisation of West Africa and the Manner in which Slaves are made. (2) On the Manner of Carrying Slaves to the West Indies. (3) On the Treatment of Slaves on the Plantations. (4) On the extent of the Trade and Population, Slave and Free, of the West Indies. (5) On the Slave Trade and Slavery as practised by other Nations. People of many callings gave evidence: former Governors, naval officers, captains of slavers, civil servants, doctors, traders, travellers. One of the travellers, Dr. Andrew Spaarman, a Swede whose accounts of Africa are still valued, told how slaves were procured:

> When the Kings of the country want slaves for the purchase of goods, they send their horsemen in the night to make as many slaves as they can. In the neighbourhood of Goree he saw one of these expeditions. The King of Barbessia came to him in the night to tell him that he was

going to send out a party to make slaves, as he wanted brandy to encourage his officers. In the course of the conversation, the King became so intoxicated with madeira, by Dr. Spaarman's bedside, that he was carried away speechless. Dr. Spaarman saw the party set out and saw them return with some slaves they had made. They conceal part . . . on these occasions, to enhance their price.

There was much factual, impartial, uncontroversial information of the same sort, and the evidence favouring Abolition was massive, almost overwhelming. On 10 April Pitt wrote to Wilberforce to fix the day for the debate. It was to be on 12 May. 'The more we consider the case, the more irresistible it is in all its parts.'

When Wilberforce duly rose to propose the motion, he spoke, before a tense House, for three hours and a half. 'I had not prepared my language', so he noted in his diary, 'or even gone over all my matter, but being well acquainted with the subject I got on.'

Understatement could scarcely go further. No exact record of what was said has survived, but echoes may be caught of an occasion of which Burke, incomparably the finest orator of his day, whose own words can still be read with the excitement with which they must have infused his hearers, remarked: 'The principles were so well laid down, and supported with so much force and order, that it equalled anything I have ever heard in modern times, and is not perhaps to be surpassed in the remains of Grecian eloquence.'

Wilberforce began by contrasting the greatness of his theme, in which the whole world, and posterity, were involved, with the insufficiency of its advocate. He took heart from the encouragement which he had already received, and reflected that 'However adverse any honourable gentleman may now be, yet we shall all be of one opinion in the end.' That, he said, gave him courage.

He did not appeal to the passions, but to 'cool and impartial reason'. He accused no one, but 'take the shame upon myself in common with the whole Parliament of Great Britain for having suffered this horrid Trade to be carried on under our authority. We are all guilty.'

The speaker next touched upon the Privy Council Report, upon the motive for the procurement of slaves, and then, in vivid passages, spoke of the actual conditions of their transport. He contrasted, ironically, one lyrical description of a typical Middle

Passage given by a certain Mr. Norris of Liverpool, with the grim facts: the slaves branded with hot irons; herded on shipboard and stowed so close 'that there is not room to tread among them, and even in a ship which wanted 200 of her complement, the stench intolerable': fed—forcibly if necessary—on horse-beans; for exercise, forced to dance and sing in their fetters, if necessary under the lash; chained together so that they were unable to end their misery by throwing themselves into the sea. As for mortality, the latest figures indicated that many died before they sailed: that an average of twelve and half per cent died on passage, and a further four and a half per cent before the day of sale. One third more perished in what was euphemistically known as 'the seasoning'—and this, said Wilberforce 'in a country exactly like their own—where they are healthy and happy—as some of the evidence would pretend'.

The influence of slaving on the mercantile marine was, so he argued, harmful, not beneficial. 'More sailors die in one year in the Slave Trade than die in two years in all our other trades put together.'

Wilberforce dealt with two more aspects: the effect of Abolition on the Planters, and in France. The West Indies, he declared, should be cultivated by free men. Prosperity, not disaster, would ensue. He had heard so often, even in his brief experience, that this or that measure would ruin commerce—it never had. 'I have shown', he said, 'that Abolition is the only possible stimulus whereby a regard for population and consequently for the happiness of the negroes can be effectively excited in those islands.' Free labourers he said, would increase and multiply—slaves would continue to need replacement by the cruel means then employed.

As for France, said Wilberforce, 'If the Slave Trade be such as I have described it, if it be in truth both wicked and impolitic, we cannot wish a greater mischief to France than that she should adopt it.' But France, he added, 'is too enlightened a nation to begin pushing a scandalous as well as a ruinous traffic at the very time when England sees her folly and gives it up'.

Imperfectly as it may have been reported, Wilberforce's closing periods should be quoted in full, since they rounded off the most famous speech he had yet made in Parliament.

I trust . . . I have proved that, upon every ground, the total abolition ought to take place. I have urged many things which are not my own leading motives for proposing it, since I have wished to show every description of gentlemen, and particularly the West India planters, who deserve every attention, that the abolition is politic upon their own principles. Policy, however, Sir, is not my principle, and I am not ashamed to say it. There is a principle above everything that is politic, and when I reflect on the command which says: 'Thou shalt do no murder,' believing its authority to be divine, how can I dare to set up any reasonings of my own against it? And, Sir, when we think of Eternity and of the future consequences of all human conduct, what is there in this life that should make any man contradict the dictates of his conscience, the principles of justice, and the laws of God?

Sir, the nature and all the circumstances of this Trade are now laid open to us. We can no longer plead ignorance. We cannot evade it. We may spurn it. We may kick it out of the way. But we cannot turn aside so as to avoid seeing it. For it is brought now so directly before our eyes that this House must decide and must justify to all the world and to its own conscience, the rectitude of the grounds of its decision. A society has been established for the abolition of this Trade, in which Dissenters, Quakers, Churchmen—in which the most conscientious men of all persuasions—have united and made common cause. Let not Parliament be the only body that is insensible to the principles of natural justice. Let us make reparation to Africa, so far as we can, by establishing a trade upon true commercial principles, and we shall soon find the rectitude of our conduct rewarded by the benefits of a regular and growing commerce.

IV

The walls of Jericho did not fall before the trumpet, though they trembled. Burke rose to support Wilberforce with all his powers of eloquence and reasoning. If some loss there must be, he said of Abolition, 'were they not prepared to pay the price of virtue?'

Pitt followed. He was willing, he said, to listen to arguments for the continuance of the Trade, but how could they be reconciled with the principles of justice and humanity? He had been told that if slavery were abolished by Great Britain, it would lead to the smuggling in of Negroes by other nations. 'Should that be the case', he said—and he spoke as Prime Minister—'our language must be that Great Britain has resources to enable her to protect her Islands, and to prevent others carrying on a traffic she has thought fit for her character and honour to abandon.'

Fox followed, warm in support, confessing his hope that France, at any rate, might be expected 'to catch a spark from the light of our fire and to run a race with us in promoting the ends of humanity'.

The adverse case produced no rhetoric. Alderman Newnham should have been laughed at, but was not, when he said that Abolition 'would render the City of London the scene of bankruptcy and ruin'. A Mr. Dempster asked whether Pitt or Fox or Wilberforce had plantations of their own, and declared that 'though sugar could indeed be cultivated more profitably by free labour than by slaves' (the very core of Wilberforce's argument), yet 'Parliament had no pretence of right to prescribe to the gentlemen of the West Indies by what hands their plantations should be cultivated'. Others followed, but it was Lord Maitland who, cleverer than most, appealed to the jealousy of the Commons on a point of privilege, and said that they would be surrendering their historical rights if they accepted the evidence given before the Privy Council, and did not insist on its being given all over again at their own Bar.

This proposal opened the prospect of delay and obstruction of every sort. But it had one advantage, and it carried the day. It would give more time, perhaps much more time, for puzzled Members, humane in sentiment, moved by Wilberforce, but disturbed by the thought that they might be harming interests other than their own, to make up their minds. It was agreed, without a division, to go into Committee on nine specified days. When those days had passed, with the evidence far from finished, Alderman Newnham himself proposed that the question should be reconsidered early in the next session. Meanwhile, the regulations of Sir William Dolben's hasty Act were amended and continued, a measure which was quickly approved.

In the interval, the Abolitionists could sound France. Charles Grey, one of the most liberal minded of the younger Whigs, wrote in answer to an appeal from Wilberforce: 'If France alone would consent to abolish this detestable and inhuman traffic, the proposed plan would not have a more zealous supporter than myself.' Many felt like Grey: all seemed agreed that, while there was no hope of Spain being joined in any measure of enlightenment, there was indeed some chance that M. Necker, who was then in office, would publicly favour a cause about which he had already written sympathetically.

V

When, in January 1790, Parliament reassembled, the hearing of evidence proceeded. The witnesses in defence of the Trade were examined first, and by April their case had been completed. Supporters of slaving then tried a daring manœuvre. Alderman Newnham rose to protest against the calling of further evidence. The House, so he argued, must by now have been convinced that Abolition was impracticable. Lord Maitland raised the bogey of a Negro rising, and for a time it seemed that a skilful ruse might succeed.

But the average run of Members, if still irresolute, were not lacking in a sense of fair play. The House decided, without a division, that the hearing of evidence should be continued. 'Our opponents, blessed be God, fairly beat', noted Wilberforce in his diary.

All through May and June the Committee for Abolition met almost daily. Wilberforce was there, watching and helping witnesses. Then he was off to Yorkshire. A General Election was imminent, and he had become almost a stranger to his constituents. But Yorkshire loyalty remained staunch: no discontent at neglect of county interests was expressed: Wilberforce was again returned with a handsome majority, and Pitt increased his hold in the House of Commons.

Wilberforce spent the rest of the summer in the country. In October he stayed with Gisborne, his Cambridge friend, at Yoxall in Staffordshire, working away at the evidence before the Commons in company with Thomas Babington, another zealot. 'The Slave Trade now occupies them nine hours daily' said a visitor staying in the same house. 'They talk of sitting up one night in each week. . . .' The strain was, in fact, beginning to tell on Wilberforce, particularly on his eyes, but he kept going.

By November, he was back in London, 'plunging at once into a dinner-circle of Cabinet Ministers'. Yet although Wilberforce had the ear of great men, on the whole the omens were unfavourable. In the country at large, the first enthusiasm had begun to lose impetus. If Pitt, Fox and Burke were still warm advocates, the Government itself, as a body, could still not be committed, while attention was for the moment largely directed to Burke's newly published attack on the principles which were beginning to dominate France. The only change for the better was that Grenville, not Sydney, was now in charge of Colonial affairs and he, so it was thought, might act as a counter-weight to Thurlow in the House of Lords.

Even Wesley felt that the task was beyond merely human capacity.

> Unless the Divine power has raised you up to be as '*Athanasius contra mundum*,' [so ran one of the last letters of his life] I see not how you can go through your glorious enterprise. . . . Unless God has raised you up for this very thing, you will be worn out by the opposition of men and devils, but if God be for you, who can be against you? . . . Go on, in the name of God, and in the power of His might, till even American slavery, the vilest that ever saw the sun, shall vanish away before it.

The debate of 1791 in fact followed much the same course as that of 1789—and to as little satisfaction. Wilberforce, Burke, Fox, Pitt, all spoke with eloquence and effect, armed as they now were with the fullest array of facts it was possible to assemble. It was no use. Property, precedent, fear—these were stronger in their power than Wilberforce's passion, Fox's humanity, Burke's brilliance, Pitt's justice. The opposition case was put, with brevity and candour, by a certain Mr. Drake, a name not inappropriate in one whose aim was to sustain a traffic encouraged by Elizabethan adventurers:

> The leaders, it is true, are for Abolition, but the minor orators, the pygmies will, I trust, carry the question against them. The property of the West Indians is at stake; and though men may be generous with their own property, they should not be so with the property of others.

Property, like law, was sacred. Members were seeing it assailed, in sinister fashion, in a neighbouring Kingdom, France. So the pygmies had it. After a two days' debate, prolonged until the early hours of the morning of 20 April, the House of Commons rejected Wilberforce's motion by 163 votes to 88. Even had the vote been less decisive than it was, it is improbable that Abolition would have had the slightest chance in the Lords, where peers held property to be as sacred as their own position in society.

Wilberforce was defeated. A less resilient man would have been crushed.

VI

The adventures of Clarkson in Paris were unexpected, but whatever the outcome of his journey had been, it is unlikely that any decision by France would have helped the cause of Abolition in England. If France had been favourable, it would have been regarded as a sign of that extreme opinion which the majority of the Commons feared and detested; if unfavourable, the fact would have afforded support to those who argued that unilateral Abolition by Great Britain would merely have helped the French trade in slaves.

The Bastille had fallen a few weeks before Clarkson's arrival. 'Men are born free and with equal rights', so ran the first article of the Declaration of Rights of Man, which also proclaimed: 'Free and equal they remain.' The statement was unequivocal: there was no talk of one principle for the white man and another for the black. In fact, the cause in which Clarkson was engaged had already found French champions, the Abbé Raynal, Sieyès Brissot, Clavière, Condorcet, Rochefoucauld, Mirabeau and Lafayette were among them: they had, indeed, established a body somewhat similar to Sharp's Committee, with the name of *Les Amis des Noirs*.

Mirabeau, startled by the information which Clarkson brought with him, ordered a model of a slave ship, loaded with its freight, as an ornament for his dining-room. Even Louis XVI expressed mild interest, though Necker, who with his wife had been among the most enthusiastic in their welcome, thought that the model itself might 'affect His Majesty too much'. He was not allowed to see it.

Despite a plethora of talk, and much private good-will, nothing happened, even after six months. Slavers, in Bordeaux and Havre, soon marshalled advocates and interests in Paris. Clavière was threatened with assassination, Clarkson denounced as an English spy. Finally, so the popular argument ran—neatly complementing certain ideas raised in the House of Commons—if France gave up the Trade before England, would not England reap the profit? And why, if she were so impassioned, did not England give a lead?

Clarkson was still in Paris when Versailles was invaded by a starving mob, and the King and Queen escorted, prisoners of the people, to the Tuileries. There followed some months of illusory calm, during which *Les Amis des Noirs* canvassed their subject. Suddenly, they were silenced. There had been a terrible outbreak of violence between parties in the Western and French portion of the island of San Domingo—uprisings, murders, massacres. The infection spread, first to Martinique and the southern French islands, then to near-by Dominica, which was British territory. The Dominica trouble, a rising of slaves, occurred in 1791, and was soon suppressed, but the terror which continued to reign in San Domingo served to clinch the matter for opponents of Abolition. They had indeed been right! If Wilberforce and his like should ever triumph, no white man could be safe in the plantations. Every event both in France and the islands showed the folly—to call it nothing worse—of pressing the case any further.

The reasoning was faulty. If anything could have increased existing dangers, it would have been fresh importation of slaves. But at this moment, reason was unpopular with legislators stiffened by the force of events abroad to resist change of any sort.

It was ironical that, at a time when the Commons had expressed itself so decidedly, the feelings of men and women in general grew increasingly favourable to the cause. For with Wilberforce's public discomfiture, popular enthusiasm began to return. A ceaseless flow of propaganda took effect. Cowper's poem, *The Negro's Complaint*, printed on the finest paper, neatly folded and superscribed *A Subject for Conversation at the Tea Table*, was circulated everywhere, and was set to music.

> *Is there, as you sometimes tell us,*
> *Is there One who rules on high;*
> *Has He bid you buy and sell us,*
> *Speaking from His throne, the sky?*
>   *Ask Him if your knotted scourges,*
>   *Fetters, blood-extorting screws,*
>   *Are the means which duty urges,*
>   *Agents of His will to use?*

This was shrewd hitting. Those who read Cowper were soon enabled
to buy a cameo devised by Josiah Wedgwood, which showed a
negro in an attitude of piteous entreaty. The ornament soon became
fashionable, inlaid in gold, on gentlemen's snuff-boxes. It did as
much as anything addressed to the intelligence to keep Abolition
fresh in mind.

VII

The next step in the campaign entailed organisation of opinion
through public meetings, which were to be followed by petitions
to the House of Commons. To a man in Wilberforce's position,
lobbying Members of Parliament was an easy matter compared with
the constant and detailed attention needed for such work, in days
when communications, though improving, were still slow, at any
rate once the traveller had left the main roads. Wilberforce was good
at organising, and his steadfast purpose helped him over difficulties.
He 'knew everybody' as the phrase was. He could offer sound advice
about the most influential men in any given neighbourhood—often
he discussed how best to humour them, to get them on the side of
right.

It was soon clear that Members of Parliament had not settled
anything by their votes in the full-dress debates which had already
taken place. Public opinion, expressed by petition, was a comparatively new element in politics. It was disturbing—for although the
unreformed House of Commons of the eighteenth century was not
truly representative (except of country gentlemen), and the
alliance between constituents and Members was not always strong,
yet such a general manifestation was bound to have the effect of
keeping conscience alive, particularly when it was known that Pitt,
and some other members of the Government, remained unshaken
in their view that it was a scandal to allow the Slave Trade to
continue another day.

The petitions were almost all on one side. There were 312 from
England and Wales, 187 from Scotland. Beyond the Border,
Abolitionists had always been strong, and they had been led from
the pulpit. Against this muster, advocates of the Trade presented

only five petitions. Two of these were from individuals, and one of the remainder was at least in favour of regulation. Perhaps the most noteworthy sign of changing times was that Liverpool itself did not petition either way. 'Liverpool will never again, I think, petition on this subject', wrote a Lancashire correspondent to Wilberforce; 'conviction of the truth has spread amongst us widely.' The writer even hinted that support of the Trade by Colonel Tarleton, the local Member, would cost him his seat at the next election.

The City of London itself returned to liberal traditions. The proposal for an anti-slavery petition made in the Common Council was stifled by the Lord Mayor and a majority of Aldermen, but they could not override a meeting of the Liverymen of the ancient Guilds. The Livery attended in full strength, drowned Aldermanic protests in groans and hisses, and triumphantly carried the motion. The gesture pleased Pitt as much as Wilberforce, for the Prime Minister depended upon the City, and never failed to pay regard to its opinion. He was less pleased with some of Wilberforce's lieutenants, Clarkson in particular. Since his visit to France, Clarkson had been unguarded in expressions sympathetic to the Revolution. By saying too much on the subject, he hurt a crusade nearer to his heart. 'I wish him better notions in politics', wrote Milner to Wilberforce. 'You will see Clarkson', said Wilberforce to Lord Muncester: 'Caution him against talking of the French Revolution; it will be the ruin of our cause.'

It had been arranged that Wilberforce would once again speak in the Commons against slavery during April 1792. Meanwhile, a few weeks earlier, a foreign ruler had given a lead. On 16 March, Christian VII of Denmark signed an edict declaring that 'with the beginning of the year 1803, all traffic in the Slave Trade by our subjects shall cease'.

This was something, though it was little more than a gesture. The Danish possessions in the West Indies were few and small. Only some fifty or sixty ships engaged in regular trade thereto. A greater drawback was the date. The edict would not become operative for more than ten years. Wilberforce, Sharp and his Committee, Pitt, Fox, Burke and Grenville, all were for immediate Abolition. They found it unendurable that the Trade should exist one unnecessary day.

The example given by Denmark, honourable as it was, had results other than were expected. It gave an handle to those who were exploring a new means of delay—Abolition by Degrees. Such people found an advocate very close to Pitt: this was Henry Dundas, later Viscount Melville, a man upon whom Pitt had long depended for practical advice. Dundas, besides being a friend, had his ear to the ground, and was regarded as one in whom common sense would never be overruled by sentiment. That very year, Wilberforce had noted in his diary: 'Went with Pitt to Wimbledon. . . . A long discussion with Dundas after dinner *tête-à-tête*—most excellent man of business. Oh, what a pity he is not alive to what is best!'

When the time came for the debate, this differed notably from those which had preceded it. Wilberforce himself created a sensation by relating how six British slave ships had recently anchored off the town of Calabar. The captains, on learning that the African slave-dealers were asking higher prices, decided to overawe them by the use of force. They opened fire, and continued a bombardment for three hours, during which time twenty people were killed and many injured. There was no answering fire, and when they closed inshore, the slavers found the factors so terrified that they consented to sell slaves at any price the captains fixed. No more brutal episode of its kind had ever been related, and the effect of the recital was electric.

When their time came, opponents, with good reason, were comparatively moderate in their expressions. Mr. Baillie, agent for Grenada, raised the San Domingo scare but did not venture to argue from principles. Colonel Tarleton, following, went so far as to say that if the Trade were not an old-established interest, he himself would be its most strenuous opponent.

Dundas turned the course of the proceedings. Was precipitant Abolition possible? he asked. Was it practical? Might it not run counter to an equally great object: 'the sacred attention which Parliament had ever shown to the interests of individuals'—and by 'individuals' he meant white men of property. He himself would favour Abolition by regulations. '*What* regulations?' interjected Fox. Regulations, said Dundas, to promote the breeding of Negroes in the West Indies; to put an end by gradual process to heredity slavery; to improve the condition of existing slaves; to provide for the education of their children. Two results would accrue: the practicability of abolishing the Trade without injury to the planters' interests would be proved by experience, and in course of time a transition would be effected from slave labour to free. Dundas amplified his theme, and concluded with an appeal to all 'gentlemen of the moderate or middle way of thinking' to work together for his idea, and thus 'reduce the question to its proper bounds'.

This was indeed the voice of common sense, of political reason. When Dundas had finished, Addington stepped down from the Speaker's chair to thank him for relieving him from the 'utmost anxiety'—torn as he had been between hatred of the Trade and respect for individual rights. Robert Jenkinson, later to become Lord Liverpool and a future Prime Minister, expressed equal gratitude. The 'gentlemen of the moderate or middle way of thinking' had heard an enticing voice. Dundas and his proposals were salves to their conscience: he was offering a way out which would offend no one—except the Negroes. But these same gentlemen had yet to hear the most formidable speeches in support of Wilberforce. They were from Fox and Pitt, political enemies, but united on this one subject.

Fox let fly at moderation. It reminded him, he said, of a passage in Middleton's *Life of Cicero:* 'To break open a man's house and kill him, his wife and his family in the night is certainly a most heinous crime and deserving of death; but even this may be done with moderation!' The real question was not whether the execrable Trade required regulation, but whether it was fit to be continued at all. And it seemed to him, that in the scheme proposed something like a foundation would be laid for preserving it for ever. 'I note the terms in which the Trade has been reprehended by the last two speakers', he added, 'but where is the proof that they will ever vote for the abolition of it?'

Meanwhile, year after year, Africans were being plundered and murdered and sold into slavery. What the country at large felt about this, they knew from evidence before them. 'I am certain of this', he said: 'The Table is never loaded with petitions but when the people of England feel an actual grievance, and when the House ought to feel itself bound to give a remedy.'

Fox's summing up was characteristic, and it certainly was not 'moderate':

> I believe the Trade to be impolitic, I know it to be inhuman. I am certain it is unjust. I find it so inhuman and unjust that, if the Colonies cannot be cultivated without it, they ought not to be cultivated at all. . . . As long as I have a voice to speak, this question shall never be at rest . . . and if I and my friends should die before they have attained their glorious object, I hope there will never be wanting men alive to do their duty, who will continue to labour till the evil shall be wholly done away.

Dundas, unmoved by this eloquence, made a few dry remarks in defence of his own position. Then, to carry the question to an issue, he moved an amendment to insert the word 'gradually' into Wilberforce's motion in favour of Abolition. He was supported by Jenkinson. Then came Pitt.

Everyone was by that time near to exhaustion. The long night full of words was nearly over, dawn not far away. 'From London to Inverness', so a friend had written to Wilberforce, 'Mr. Pitt's sincerity is questioned; and unless he can convince the nation of his cordiality in our cause, his popularity must suffer greatly.' Wilberforce, who knew Pitt as well as any man, did not share these doubts, did not believe the Prime Minister would be deflected from his purpose by the events of San Domingo, by Clarkson's indiscretions, or by any other circumstance. His judgment was right. Pitt delivered one of the greatest and certainly the noblest speech of his life, dispelling all doubts, and holding the weary audience spellbound by his mastery of the subject; still more, perhaps, by his way of carrying the theme back to its foundation.

First he went straight to the main contention of the 'moderates' that a gradual, distant Abolition would seem the best interests of the planters. Immediate action, he said, would compel them to improve conditions, and so increase the numbers and labour of their Negroes. It would help their finances by reducing their debts which—it was admitted—were due to speculation in slaves. It would minimise the danger of insurrection, which arose largely from contact of newly imported Negroes with more resigned slaves:

> Surely, when gentlemen talk so vehemently of the safety of the Islands and charge us with being so indifferent to it, when they speak of the

calamities of San Domingo and of similar dangers impending on their
own heads, it ill becomes them to cry out for further importation. . . .
Let us vote that the Abolition of the Slave Trade shall be immediate.
Will my right honourable friends answer for the safety of the islands
during any imaginable intervening period?

As for the argument of property, Pitt pointed out that every new
commercial regulation, every tax, any duty levied, affected some
man's property, some man's expectations. If, on that ground,
Abolition was forbidden to Parliament, so were all fiscal measures.
And, he added, it would be particularly offensive to suppose that
Parliament had ever bound itself to maintain such a scandal as the
Slave Trade. 'As well might an individual think himself bound by a
promise to commit an assassination.' Moreover, what of the Act of
George II which forbade any master of a ship to carry off Negroes
from Africa 'by fraud, force or violence, or by any indirect practice
whatever'. That act was a dead letter, yet it still continued to be the
law, and nothing but Abolition could prevent the law from being
broken.

'And now, Sir,' said Pitt, 'I come to Africa.' What had Great
Britain done for Africa, save to rob her of thousands of her people
every year?

> Long as that Continent has been known to navigators, the extreme line
> of its coasts is all with which Europe is yet become acquainted. . . .
> Africa is known to you only in its skirts; yet even there you are able to
> inject a poison which penetrates to its very centre, corrupting every
> part to which it reaches. . . . What astonishing, I had almost said, what
> irreparable mischief have we brought upon that Continent. . . . How
> shall we hope to obtain, if it be possible, forgiveness from Heaven for
> the enormous ills we have committed, if we refuse to make use of those
> means which the mercy of Providence has still preserved us for wiping
> away the shame and guilt with which we are now covered?

Pitt briefly dismissed the argument that the Trade, if relinquished by
Britain, would be absorbed by other countries. Would France take
it on, in the light of San Domingo? Would Spain, Portugal, Holland?
'From what branch of their commerce will they draw together a
fund to feed this monster?'

Once more he returned to Africa. It was for Britain to make
amends. Let no one say that Africa 'labours under a natural

incapacity for civilisation'. Human sacrifice, he said, had once been practised in these islands, and Britons had been sold for slaves in Rome. A Roman senator might with equal justice have referred to 'British barbarians', adding, 'There is a people that will never rise to civilisation—there is a people never destined to be free.'

It was now nearly seven o'clock in the morning. Weary faces were now haggard—but still they sat enthralled.

> If we listen to the voice of reason and duty [Pitt concluded] and pursue this day the line of conduct which they prescribe, some of us may live to see the reverse of that picture from which we now turn our eyes with shame and regret. We may live to behold the natives of Africa engaged in the calm occupations of industry, in the pursuit of a just and legitimate commerce. We may behold the beams of science and philosophy breaking in upon their land, which, at some happy period, in still later times, may blaze with full lustre, and, joining their influence with that of pure religion, may illuminate and invigorate the most distant extremities of that immense Continent. . . .

Pitt declared that he would vote against Dundas's amendment, and would oppose any proposal which 'may tend to prevent or even to postpone for an hour the total abolition of the Slave Trade'.

Wilberforce, who had himself suggested to Pitt the theme of Africa, said that for the last twenty minutes his friend 'really seemed to be inspired'. Fox, Grey and Windham agreed that the speech was one of the most outstanding displays of eloquence they had ever heard. But when all was over, back came Members' fears, back came their ingrained love of compromise. Dundas's amendment, 'That the Slave Trade ought to be gradually abolished', was carried by 230 votes to 85.

VIII

Sanguine as ever, and a politician since his early manhood, Wilberforce was not as disappointed at the way the debate had gone as were some of his less experienced friends.

Reform was always slow—sometimes intolerably so. Had not Hanway and Porter agitated from 1760 to 1788 for a Regulating Act to control the exploitation of children as chimney-sweeps? The Act

7   WILLIAM COWPER
From a portrait by Lemuel F. Abbott, 1792

8   GRANVILLE SHARP
From a portrait by
George Dance

9   JAMES RAMSAY
From a portrait by
C. F. von Breda, 1789

had been duly passed, though no one was bold enough to say that the abuses did not continue.

In fact, much had been gained. The House had formally condemned the Trade. Abolition, even if not immediate, was the goal intended. Yet there were one or two who saw matters less cheerfully; Milner was among them. Writing to Wilberforce from his deanery at Carlisle he said:

> I thought of you most unremittingly the whole day of April 2 and a good deal of the night, which to me was a very restless one. . . . I think there can be no doubt that you have gained some ground . . . as far as respects public opinion; the opposers are plainly over-awed and ashamed. The worst circumstance is this Dundas—nobody thinks well of him—duplicity and artifice are esteemed parts of his character—he is judged to do what he does unwillingly and with design—in the worst sense.

While the letter was on its way, regulations for the Trade were debated, and the date for Abolition fixed for the year 1796. 'I have much cause for thankfulness', wrote Wilberforce, as indeed he had. 'We are to contend for the number of slaves to be imported—and *then for the House of Lords.*'

Even as he underlined the words, Wilberforce's spirits must have sunk. The obstructionists still had trump cards in their hands. One of them was the King, who used to chaff Wilberforce about his 'black clients', but who had now become a champion of the Trade. Others were peers on both sides of the Upper House: men like Thurlow, enemies of every liberal idea.

The Lords debate of 3 May was distinguished by the maiden speech of the King's naval son, the Duke of Clarence, afterwards to become William IV. This young man had distinguished himself in the navy by sternness to subordinates and indiscipline when orders from superiors went contrary to his own wishes. He had served in the West Indies with Nelson.

> He had been an attentive observer of the state of the negroes, and had no doubt but that he could bring forward proofs to convince their lordships that their state was far from being miserable: on the contrary that, when the various ranks of society were considered, they were comparatively in a state of humble happiness.

Nelson had recently sent him an account, complete with figures, of the plight of the labourers at his own home in Norfolk. William, though he had not given the letter much attention, may have been thinking of it when he made use of his last expression. 'Humble happiness' certainly gave the Abolitionists a wry laugh.

> An implicit obedience to the House of Commons [the Duke continued], much as I respect that House, would make the House of Peers useless, and thus the natural and constituent balance in the constitution would be endangered.

The peers had no need for such a lead. They had decided, on Thurlow's suggestion, on hearing all the evidence anew for themselves. The tactics of obstruction were to be pressed to the limit. Grenville protested vigorously, declaring that the removal of a national disgrace admitted of no delay. It was useless. Seven witnesses were heard, at such intervals as the whole House could spare, and then on 5 June, two days before the session closed, it was resolved to continue the hearing of evidence in the following year.

> Sentence had been pronounced [wrote Sir Reginald Coupland in his account of the debates]. A hundred thousand natives of West Africa had been condemned to death or penal servitude. Before another witness could attest their sufferings in the House of Lords, war had broken out between Great Britain and France. And year after year now, it was less and less possible for English ears to hear the far, faint cry of Africa beyond the guns in Europe.

3 THE GUNS OF EUROPE

WILBERFORCE'S experience as a politician would in any case have prevented him from suffering the extremes of disappointment which afflicted some of his more sanguine friends at the check to their cause in Parliament. He remained cheerful, though he must have wondered whether the span of a single lifetime was long enough to induce change in the thought of the ruling classes: most of them were as opposed to reform in such matters as the franchise as they were reluctant in support of wider claims. Moreover, he soon had proof of the violence sometimes developed by the other side. He was physically threatened by a slaver captain, Kimber, who had been tried for the murder of a Negro girl and—as Wilberforce thought—wrongfully acquitted. One of Wilberforce's friends, Lord Rokeby, insisted on sharing his coach, on a journey to York-shire, with a pistol in his pocket, so obvious was the danger.

When attending Parliament, Wilberforce had by this time exchanged the amenities of a Wimbledon retreat for a house at Clapham. It was even nearer to Westminster, and it was still refreshingly rural. From 1792 onwards he shared a house, Battersea Rise, with his friend, kinsman and fellow-Yorkshireman Henry Thornton. One of their neighbours was Edward Eliot, who had married Pitt's favourite sister, and another was Charles Grant. Thornton was a banker, who was at one time Governor of the Bank of England; Grant had made a fortune in the Orient and was a

Director of the East India Company. This group formed part of
what became known as the Clapham Sect. The members were
wealthy, influential, practical, Evangelical, and given to charitable
causes. They have lately found an enchanting historian in Mr. E. M.
Forster, great-nephew of Henry Thornton's daughter, Marianne.
She herself recorded some valuable glimpses of Wilberforce, his
ways, and his family:

> He was as restless and as volatile as a child, and during the long and
> grave discussions that went on between him and my father and others,
> he was most thankful to refresh himself by throwing a ball or a bunch
> of flowers at me, or opening the glass door and going off for a race on
> the lawn, 'to warm his feet'. . . . His love for and enjoyment in all
> children was remarkable.

Milner confirmed this 'volatility' in his friend. 'Now, Wilberforce,
listen', he would command, 'for no power will make me repeat
what I am going to say!' Such used to be his exclamation when his
friend was flitting after a child, a cat, a flower or a new book,
just when the pair had something important to discuss. Wilberforce
would duly listen: Milner always had something sensible to say.
Then he would be off. In fact, he had need of all the distraction
possible, for there was evidence of approaching crisis both at home
and abroad. Many shrewd judges even thought that revolution was
a possibility, so general was distress, so intoxicating the ideas drifting
across the Channel. Then French excesses grew outrageous, causing
such a reaction in Britain that the likelihood of war between the
two countries became real and immediate. The massacres in Paris
of September 1792, the opening of the Scheldt by the French in
violation of international Treaty which reserved its navigation to
the Dutch, who were Britain's allies, and the execution of Louis XVI
in January 1793 brought matters to a head.

In the month of February suspense was ended. The French
Republic declared war on England and Holland, and Members of
Parliament were spared the painful necessity of making up their
minds whether it was right or politic to mobilise against a nation of
fanatics. Pitt's budget speech of a year earlier, when he had prophesied
the continuance of peace for another fifteen years, was shown to be
as unrealistic as so many forecasts before and since that time; nor
was the fact of war altogether unpopular. A decree of the French

Convention had already 'offered assistance to all people who wish to recover their liberty', thus inviting the formation of what is now known as a fifth column in every European country. Unfortunately for France, such a declaration had the effect of hardening opinion wherever it might have been inclined to waver, while she soon made it plain that Burke's alarms had not been exaggerated, and that the Revolution, if it had released ideas valuable to mankind, had also brought dregs to the surface. It was, indeed, chiefly the reactionary folly and the military ineptitude of opponents that allowed France first to defend her own frontiers successfully by force of arms, and then set her on a career of conquest in which her success was more apparent than application of her own principles.

As Burke eloquently put it, France was 'not a new Power of an old kind' but 'a new Power of a new species. The Revolution was made, not to set France free, but to make her formidable: not to make her a neighbour, but a mistress; not to make her observant of laws, but to put her in a condition to impose them.'

Immediately before the outbreak of war, and for some years afterwards, there was real alarm in the United Kingdom at the possibility of disturbance inside as well as outside the country, quite apart from those recurring troubles in Ireland which seemed inseparable from the Protestant ascendancy in that misgoverned island. Measures of repression were used by Pitt which have brought some odium upon him, since in the light of history they appear to have been unnecessary. This is hind-sight. What was visible was ferment; the foundation of political clubs and combinations which, since they were an unfamiliar ingredient in English life, caused deep concern. Such explosive anti-Christian works as Thomas Paine's *Rights of Man* found such an avid public that a million and a half copies are said to have been circulated. Moreover, the anti-Catholic riots of 1780, instigated by Lord George Gordon, when for days London was at the mercy of a wrecking mob, were still a vivid memory. That same mob, living in squalor on the edge of starvation, were an ever-present reminder to those with possessions, of a seething, unhappy world at once close to and remote from all which, to those with a stake in the country, made life agreeable.

I will frankly own [so Wilberforce had written at the close of 1792] that I entertain rather gloomy apprehensions concerning the state of

the country. Not that I fear any speedy commotion—of this I own I see
no danger. Almost every man of property in the Kingdom is, of course,
the friend of civil order, and if a few mad-headed professors of liberty
and equality were to attempt to bring their theories into practice, they
would be crushed in an instant. But yet I do foresee a gathering storm,
and I cannot help fearing that a country which, like this, has so long
been blessed beyond all example with every spiritual and temporal
good, will incur those judgements of an incensed God which in the
Prophets are often denounced against those who forget the Author of
all their mercies.

These were wise words: sober, not alarmist. They might have been
written by Wesley, who had actually said: 'The greater the share
the people have in government, the less liberty, civil or religious,
does a nation enjoy.' Wesley's immense service to the continuing
political stability of the country, by his urging on the poor the
hard-working, selfless, abstinent life, with a reward in the hereafter,
was too little appreciated in the very classes whose ascendancy he
supported. They alone were the proper target for Wilberforce's
charge of lack of gratitude both to God and to the influences which
kept them in control.

Meanwhile, war directed men's thoughts overseas, for at first, as
so often, Britain's effort fell mainly upon her Navy. Two fleets were
got together. Hood was sent to the Mediterranean, where, with
some help from Spaniards and Neapolitans, he was able to hold
Toulon as a Royalist enclave, though before long, thanks mainly
to the skill of a young officer of artillery, Napoleon Bonaparte, he
was forced to withdraw, the port becoming a scene of massacre.

In the Channel and Atlantic, chief command was given to Lord
Howe, and in the summer of 1794, on the glorious First of June,
Howe, by a tactical success against Villaret-Joyeuse, was able to lay
the foundations of that supremacy which Britain never lost throughout the course of the oceanic struggle. Even so, he did not prevent a
convoy of grain from America from reaching starving France, and
the battle was memorable more for its long-term than for its
immediate effects. It was made, none the less, a great occasion. Six
prizes were brought in to Spithead. George III visited the ships in
person with his family, and presented his favourite admiral with a
jewelled sword.

For many outside Court circles, the return of Howe's ships, of which timely notice was given, provided a chance not only to pay tribute to the Navy upon which the safety of the realm depended, but to gain an idea of the conditions of war, if not quite at first hand, then at no far remove. Wilberforce seized upon it. As soon as the fleet had anchored, he was off along the Portsmouth Road with Henry Thornton and Charles Grant on a trip he might be envied.

The relevant entries in his diary—characteristically breathless—ran as follows:

> June 25. To Portsmouth and saw the Gambiers — 26th. Rowed in a revenue boat to the prizes; then to Spithead (firing grand). The *Queen* and *Defence*, where pleasing confabulation with Gambier—then valiant Captain Pringle, where ate—then *Queen*, where dined—sea scene—officers civil—afterwards got off when the ladies did—saw the Ship—marine officers and sailors—characteristic manners. Rowed to Haslar Hospital, where saw our poor wounded—Gambier well spoken of. Terrible appearance of the men blown up. Home and Gambier's. Portsmouth Point—wickedness and blasphemy abounds—shocking scene. 27th to Forton prison, where much talk with French prisoners; true democrats; saw their wounded—and then off to London. . . .

The *Queen*, where the visitors dined, had worn the flag of Alan Gardner in the battle, but had suffered cruelly, her captain dying of his wounds. Wilberforce's particular friend James Gambier, known as 'Preaching Jemmy', was as formidable in attack as he was at prayer. He had done splendidly in action commanding the *Defence*, in which he had broken the French line, and he was to be given the King's gold medal. So was Pringle, in the ship rightly named the *Valiant*. As for Portsmouth Point, it presented a scene rendered most characteristically by the ebullient Rowlandson. On this occasion it was viewed by graver eyes, by a party of sober Parliamentarians who had been given a glimpse of that private and extraordinary world inhabited by the officers and men of the sailing Navy. Incidentally, it was a world full of Abolitionists, including Gambier and Thomas Trotter, the Physician to the Fleet.

II

War against the King's enemies was one thing; differences with friends another. Yet it is notorious that war may exacerbate private differences and may even make honest divergencies of view appear unpatriotic. It was so now, when it became clearer month by month that Pitt, so secure in his position as Parliamentary leader, had little of his father's genius as a strategist. War had, in fact, forced Pitt to realise that his hopes for a long era of peace and financial prosperity could not be revived, and that if he remained in office it would be because there was no man better able to unite the country behind him. It brought him no other compensation.

At first, war drew Wilberforce closer to his friend than ever. No one, not of Cabinet rank, could have been nearer the centre of affairs, more trusted with secrets, better able to uplift the spirits of those on whom responsibility lay.

> I am convinced [wrote Wilberforce of Pitt], if the flame of pure disinterested patriotism burns in any human bosom, it does in his. I am convinced, and that on long experience and close observation, that in order to benefit his country he would give up not situation merely and emolument, but what in his case is much more, personal credit and reputation, though he knew that no human being would ever become acquainted with the sacrifice he should have made.

All the same, and despite this 'language of the heart', the affairs of the nation, particularly abroad, appeared to grow increasingly unfavourable. War disrupted trade. In Europe, the conditions of such allies as England then had went from bad to worse. Belgium was occupied: the French soon overran Holland, forced the States-General to sue for peace. Was it right for statesmen, and for Christians, to persist in a course out of which so little good seemed to come?

The matter was further complicated by what was happening in the West Indies. With a strong Navy, the most obvious points for attack were the distant French islands, to secure which Pitt sent expeditions which were expensive in man-power, chiefly owing to the unhealthy climate. There was this to justify the effort: the tropical 'sugar islands' were then regarded as the richest plums of Empire. If French possessions in the Caribbean could be seized and kept, it would not only deprive the foe of an important branch of commerce, but repay Great Britain much of the cost of the war.

The position of the French colonists had in fact gone from bad to worse. Royalist and Revolutionary factions in the islands still warred savagely, and the National Assembly in Paris, affronted by the resolve of some of the colonists to sever ties with France, jumped the stage of abolishing the Slave Trade by decreeing the abolition of slavery itself, in the hope that liberated Negroes would extirpate the Royalists and defend the islands from attacks by sea, in the interests of the Republican Government.

Had Wilberforce been a blind fanatic, he might have rejoiced at such an action on the part of France, but he was not deceived. It was a hasty, ill-considered measure, not a reasoned act of humanity. It was a gesture of policy, and a desperate one, not a grand resolve in the interest of Negro freedom. It settled nothing, and it merely served to increase the chances of insurrection by the slaves in British possessions. It made the task of acquiring French territory little, if any, easier.

The impact of events on the Continent, and on the far side of the Atlantic, weighed more and more heavily on the mind of a man of independence, sympathetic to but not a member of the Government, one who, in his differing way, was as patriotic as Pitt himself. Perhaps inevitably, therefore, Wilberforce was drawn by stages into opposition to the war. This fact damped his hitherto eager discussions with Pitt, and brought censure upon him.

'Perhaps my differing from Pitt', was his private comment, 'by lessening my popularity and showing me my comparative insignificance, may not be bad for me in spiritual things.' It was the remark of a humble man as well as that of a religious one, and he was, indeed, shortly to put the matter to the test.

In December 1794, after earnest consultation with such old friends as Thornton and Lord Muncaster, Wilberforce took a decisive step. In what he himself described as 'a very incoherent speech; good arguments, but all in heaps for want of preparation' he spoke in opposition to Pitt's policy on the Floor of the House of Commons, declaring that:

> It is advisable and expedient to endeavour to restore the blessings of peace upon just and reasonable terms. . . . If such efforts should be rendered ineffectual by the violence and ambition of the enemy . . . the burdens and evils of a just and necessary war will be borne with cheerfulness by a loyal, affectionate and united people.

The terms of the proposal may appear, at this distance of time, mild and even considerate to the Government. They did not seem so

then. The very fact of a public difference between Wilberforce and
Pitt, who had stood so long together, caused such a sensation that
Fox at one time had hopes that Wilberforce might be induced to
throw in his lot with the Opposition.

The personal effect was astonishing. The King cut Wilberforce at
the first *levée* he attended after his speech. 'Your friend Mr.
Wilberforce', said Windham to Lady Spencer with exaggerated
irony, 'will be happy any morning to hand you to the guillotine.'
Even Burke, now nearing the end of his life, but fierce as ever in
his detestation of French policy, could not resist a sarcasm. 'Mr.
Wilberforce is a very respectable gentleman', he said, 'but he is not
the people of England.' And for once, Yorkshire was not behind her
Member. When Wilberforce made a tour of the county in the
summer of 1795 he found resentment smouldering. 'In one family
of my most zealous partisans', he said, 'the ladies would scarcely
speak to me.'

Although Wilberforce had shown moral courage, it appeared all
too likely that his step might have been unfortunate. He might, so
it was thought, become the tool of unscrupulous men. Meanwhile
his action had shaken all who had admired his hitherto irreproach-
able loyalty to Pitt. 'I can truly say', wrote Milner from Carlisle 'I
never was so much concerned about politics in my life.' Milner
always spoke rough sense, and he privately deplored what Wilberforce had done: nevertheless, he was the first to defend him when,
as happened in Cambridge and elsewhere, his friend's personal
reputation was attacked.

Wilberforce, as a sociable, loyal and affectionate man, felt his
position acutely. He could not, with honesty, regret his statement,
but its cost was high. 'Party of *the old firm* at the Speaker's; I
not there': so he noted sadly in February 1795. Exile was hard:
fortunately it did not last.

III

There were only three occasions in Pitt's public life, so he told a
friend towards its close, when events had caused him loss of sleep.
The first of them was on his difference with Wilberforce; the second

was at the time of the naval mutiny of the Nore; the third was when news was brought to him of Nelson's death at Trafalgar.

When it was clear beyond question that there was not the slightest danger of Wilberforce becoming a settled opponent of his policy, and when Pitt had had more time to reflect on the strength of that opinion which had led Wilberforce to express his wish for peace, the breach was half healed. Pitt began to appreciate the sagacity of his old friend as well as his integrity, and after a little awkwardness they revived their fellowship. Pettiness had no place in such characters.

On 21 March 1795 the two met at a dinner-party. 'I think both meaning to be kind to each other,' noted Wilberforce, 'both a little embarrassed.' A few weeks later, Wilberforce paid a call at Downing Street, finding Pitt laid up with gout; and on 25 April, Edward Eliot was the bridge between them. 'Called Eliot's', so Wilberforce noted, 'knowing that Pitt was there, and that Pitt knew I knew it, and thinking, therefore, that it would seem unkind not to do it.'

Matters were made increasingly smooth by Pitt's rising pacifism. 'All Pitt's supporters,' Wilberforce noted in May, 'believe him disposed to make peace.' So much was this so that Thurlow actually laid a bet of five guineas with the Dukes of Leeds and Bedford that Pitt would vote with Wilberforce when Wilberforce moved a new peace resolution. A few days later, all was as of old. Wilberforce noted that Pitt, with himself, Eliot and another friend, had spent a summer afternoon together at Battersea Rise, 'walking, foining, laughing and reading verses as before'. The rare recurrence of the old word 'foining' did indeed show harmony restored.

Yet if private peace was regained, the world struggle seemed as all-pervasive and as unsatisfactory as ever, while Pitt's political friends, Grenville, Windham and Dundas in particular, were not nearly so forgiving as their chief. They became more so after Wilberforce had enjoyed a personal triumph in Yorkshire. There, he had boldly outfaced opponents of new repressive measures by a Government which had become alarmed by increasing signs of unrest, chiefly the result of bad harvests and trade depression. Popular opprobrium fell upon Pitt, and there was even an outbreak against the King as he drove to Westminster to open Parliament. The royal coach was damaged, and the Sovereign's person had at one time seemed in some danger. George III faced the incident with his usual courage, and escaped without hurt.

The London mob had clamoured, among other things, for peace. Unpopular war ministers were no new thing, as North had known at the time of the American War. In fact, so far was Pitt from being senselessly bellicose that throughout the years 1796 and 1797 peace might have come about had France been willing to negotiate on anything like reasonable terms. But she saw no inducement to do so. The war was still going well for her. Spain, from being an enemy, had become an ally, and had a large navy. Even the Revolutionary finances survived apparent ruin.

Against French successes, England could show little. It was true that, on Valentine's Day 1797, Jervis won a splendid victory against the Spaniards off Cape St. Vincent, but when the news reached England, it scarcely relieved the gloom resulting from the suspension of cash payments by the Bank of England. This seemed to portend a general financial crash. The crisis passed, but it was succeeded first by mutiny at Spithead, discipline being restored without bloodshed by the intercession of Lord Howe, and then by a far more serious outbreak which for critical weeks immobilised the Nore command.

Then came news of Napoleon's lightning campaign in Italy, and the withdrawal of the British Fleet from the Mediterranean, an act which seemed to Nelson and other seasoned officers a crowning humiliation. What hope was there of peace with honour when the enemy was so strong, when Bonaparte had himself been sent to survey the northern ports with a view to invasion? Lord Malmesbury indeed went to Paris on two abortive missions, making tedious journeys over neglected roads. No wonder, sneered Burke, that his progress was so slow, 'for he went all the way on his knees'.

Apart from its public aspects, the year 1797 was notable for two events in Wilberforce's private life. The first was his marriage; the second was the publication of a book which he had been contemplating for many years.

At the age of thirty-seven, the bachelor—nobody ever called Wilberforce 'settled'—fell deeply in love. The object of his devotion was Barbara Spooner. She was the eldest daughter of Isaac Spooner of Elmdon Hall, Warwickshire, a man who had made a fortune in Birmingham.

Earlier biographies of Wilberforce say little of his wife, except to emphasise the obvious, that the marriage was happy. By good fortune, the sharp eyes and attentive ears of Marianne Thornton now enable posterity to know a little more. Marianne remembered Mrs. Wilberforce well; her mother was one of her closest friends, and the character given is surprising.

> She fell in love very suddenly [wrote Marianne of Barbara Spooner], being the only religious member of a worldly family, and she confided to Mr. Wilberforce all her persecutions and difficulties. She was extremely handsome and in some ways very clever, but very deficient in common sense, a woman with narrow views and selfish aims, that is, if selfishness can be so called when it took the shape of idolatry of her husband, and thinking everything in the world ought to give way to what she thought expedient for him.
>
> Instead of helping him forward in the great works which it appeared Providence had given him to do, she always considered she was hardly used when he left her side, and instead of making his home attractive to the crowds of superior people that he invited, her love of economy made her anything but an hospitable hostess. Yet the oddity and queerness of the scenes that went on there often made up, especially to young people, for all their deficiencies.

Marianne's mother used to add that 'no one would have known how much of an angel there was in Wilberforce if they had not seen his behaviour to one whose different tastes must have tried his patience so much'.

It may well have been the preparation of Wilberforce's book which helped to bring the pair together, for this appeared shortly before his marriage, and created an unexpected stir. Unexpected, because its nature was not calculated to excite. The title was: *A Practical View of the Prevailing Religious System of Professed Christians in the Higher and Middle Classes in this Country Contrasted with Real Christianity*. The book itself was exactly that. Its main object, Wilberforce explained was:

> Not to convince the sceptic or to answer the arguments of persons who avowedly oppose the fundamental doctrines of our religion; but to point out the scanty and erroneous system of the bulk of those who belong to the class of orthodox Christians, and to contrast their defective scheme with a representation of what the author apprehends to be real Christianity.

Emphasis was as much upon the next world as upon this. The author's wish was to recall what to him was the plainest fact of all, that 'this present scene, with all its cares and all its gaieties, will soon be rolled away', and that we must 'stand before the judgement seat of Christ'. Nothing was more apparent, or sadder, than Society's 'utter forgetfulness of its being the great business of life to secure our admission into Heaven, and to prepare our hearts for its service and enjoyments'.

The supreme value of Christianity, said Wilberforce, was its direct hostility to selfishness, which he called 'the moral distemper of political communities'. Warming to his theme in a way in which Wesley would have approved, the author continued:

> In whatever class or order of society Christianity prevails, she sets herself to counteract the particular mode of selfishness to which that class is liable. Affluence she teaches to be liberal and beneficient; authority to bear its faculties with meekness and to consider the various cares and obligations belonging to its elevated station as being conditions on which that station is conferred. Thus, softening the glare of wealth and moderating the insolence of power, she renders the inequalities of the social state less galling to the lower orders, whom she instructs, in their turn, to be diligent, humble, patient: reminding them that their more lowly path has been allotted to them by the hand of God; that it is their part faithfully to discharge its duties, and contentedly to bear its inconveniences; that the present state of things is very short . . . that the peace of mind which religion offers indiscriminately to all ranks affords more true satisfaction than all the expensive pleasures which are beyond the poor man's reach . . . and finally that all human distinctions will soon be done away, and the true followers of Christ will all, as children of the same Father, be alike admitted to the possession of the same Heavenly inheritance.

This was not cant, but conviction. Wilberforce, resuming the old theme which had caused him, years before, to instigate his Proclamation Society against the vices of the time, ended with a sentence to which he gave the emphasis of italics:

> It would be an instance in myself of that very false shame which I have condemned in others, if I were not boldly to avow my firm persuasion that *to the decline of Religion and Morality our national difficulties must, both directly and indirectly, be chiefly ascribed; and that my only solid hopes for the well-being of my Country depend, not so much on her fleets and armies, not so much on the wisdom of her rulers or the spirit of her people, as on the*

persuasion that she still contains many who love and obey the Gospel of Christ; that their intercessions may yet prevail; that, for the sake of these, Heaven may still look upon us with an eye of favour.

When Wilberforce submitted his book to the publisher, Thomas Cadell, whose firm had in earlier days issued Johnson's *Lives of the Poets*, the project was not warmly received. Mr. Cadell considered that the demand for literature of a religious kind was on the decline. This was a time-honoured gambit in his profession. At once it damped expectations, and caused the author to regard the firm as benefactors if an exception should be made, and an offer put forward to issue the work under discussion.

'He evidently regarded me', said Wilberforce of Cadell, 'as an amiable enthusiast.' 'You mean to put your name to the work?' Cadell asked. Wilberforce admitted that this was so. 'Ah', said the publisher, 'then I *think* we may venture on 500 copies.' Faith was rewarded. The five hundred were sold out in a few days. By the midsummer of 1797 impressions totalling 7,500 had been disposed of, and the book was still selling briskly. It continued in demand for many years, and in due time it was translated into the principal languages of Europe—French included.

'The bishops in general', wrote Henry Thornton to Zachary Macaulay, a fellow-member of the Clapham Sect, 'much approve of it, though some more warmly, some more coldly.' Coldness was unreasonable, since Wilberforce, as a lay preacher, was at work in the cause on behalf of which they drew their stipends. 'I deem it', wrote Newton, 'the most valuable and important publication of the present age, especially as it is yours.' Arthur Young, the agriculturalist, 'read it again and again, and it made so much impression upon me that I scarcely knew how to lay it aside'. 'If I live', said the dying Burke, 'I shall thank Wilberforce for having sent such a book into the world.'

Perhaps the oddest tribute came from Sheridan, never one of Wilberforce's more obvious admirers. Sheridan, so someone told Byron, was found by a watchman in the street one dark night, 'fuddled and bewildered and almost insensible'. 'Who are *you*, Sir' said the man. No answer. 'What's your name?'—a hiccup. 'What's your name?' he asked once more. The reply, when at last it came, was solemn and impressive—'*Wilberforsssh.*'

IV

Better prospects for the country seemed to open with Nelson's destruction of the battle squadron of Bonaparte's eastern expedition (which was then overrunning Egypt) among the shoals of Aboukir Bay. It was the most spectacular feat in naval annals. News of the success reached London in October 1798, and the town was illuminated.

> Almighty God has blessed his Majesty's Arms in the late Battle, by a great Victory over the Fleet of the Enemy, who I attacked at sunset on the 1st of August, off the Mouth of the Nile.

The opening words of the Admiral's despatch soon rang through Europe.

The ascription of triumph to the Almighty was not lost upon Wilberforce, who wrote to Hannah More: 'Are you not almost as delighted with Nelson's letter as with the victory itself?' Nelson, like Milton before him, believed in 'God's Englishmen', and was not ashamed to say so. He was a clergyman's son, and the act which impressed his opponents most, after they had tasted the effects of his gunnery, was the way in which services of thanksgiving were conducted in every ship after the battle. Frenchmen at least had the consolation of reflecting that they had been overcome, not, as appeared to be the fact, by a force inferior in weight of metal to themselves, but by supernatural intervention.

Less encouraging, at least to Wilberforce, were affairs in more distant parts of Africa. While it was true that the war had caused some interruption in the trade in Negroes, it still continued, and although Wilberforce had been assiduous in his motions in the House of Commons, all measures of alleviation had been blocked either there or in the Lords, where on one occasion the Duke of Clarence had had the temerity to say of the promoters of Abolition 'that they are either fanatics or hyprocrites, and in one of those classes I rank Mr. Wilberforce'. He had been soundly rebuked by Grenville, and had the grace to apologise.

Wilberforce had never ceased to press for the cause which remained nearest his heart, but the times were increasingly against him. Ministers were distracted by pressure of war, and he was forced into guerrilla tactics. They were not ineffectual. They kept the question alive, so much so that Wilberforce remained convinced that one day (perhaps when he least expected it) the golden moment would come, and all would at last be conceded.

At least no one could suppose that he himself had slackened in his ardour. His marriage certainly did not affect it, and his wife learnt soon enough that his attention had to be wooed, even by those he loved. He had warned her of the preoccupations and worries of his political life, and these warnings were not without reason. A week was all he could spare for his honeymoon, which was spent partly in a visit to Hannah More's schools, and he was then back in his place in the House of Commons. 'My dearest wife bears my hurrying way of life with great sweetness,' said an appreciative husband, 'but it would be a sort of gaol-delivery to her no less than to myself to escape from this bustling town.'

Wilberforce was so confirmed a Parliamentarian that he believed measures of policy could be effected only through debate and voting, but, just as he had been ready to mobilise opinion to his cause in the way of petition, he never neglected other and quite different means of alleviating the lot of the Negroes. In one of them he had the fullest help from the Clapham Sect.

Ever since the Mansfield judgment, the problem of the freed Negro had grown. Many remained in the paid service of their former masters, but some did not, and when, after the American War, a number who had served with the British forces on land and sea were demobilised, some in Nova Scotia, some in the Bahamas, some in London, it was a question how best to employ their services, or, at worst, keep them from want. Private charity was then the principal means for their relief, and Granville Sharp, among other philanthropists, supported, out of his own slender means, regular pensioners.

In 1786 a certain Dr. Sleathman, who had lived for some years at the foot of the mountains of Sierra Leone, on the West Coast of Africa, suggested that indigent negroes should be transported from London and settled there as a colony in their native Africa—it would be, as it were, the slave trade in reverse.

In the spring of 1787, some hundreds of Negroes, and sixty whites, were landed at Sierra Leone. A block of fertile coast-land, about twenty miles square, was ceded by a local king to the British Crown, and work was begun on the building of a small town. But matters did not prosper: fever raged, many settlers died. Two years later came another blow. One of the inevitable petty conflicts incidental to the Slave Trade had led to the destruction of a neighbouring chief's village by British sailors. In revenge, the chief burnt the colonists' settlement.

Undiscouraged, the promoters formed a 'St. George's Bay Association' for 'opening and establishing a trade in the natural productions of Africa'. In 1791 it was given a Charter, and was incorporated by Act of Parliament as the Sierra Leone Company. Sharp was president, Thornton, chairman, Grant and Wilberforce were among the first directors. 'The design is noble', wrote Wilberforce to Wyvill, 'and I trust it will please God to bless the undertaking.'

With such experienced men in control, matters began to look up. Money was raised. Settlers were brought over from Nova Scotia, and a capital was built at Freetown. A church, a hospital, schools and warehouses sprang up. But there were still difficulties—malaria, 'incredible swarms of ants', and refractory Negroes, who preferred idleness to working—even for themselves. Then, in 1793, the Clapham friends sent out Zachary Macaulay from within their own ranks, and upon him and one colleague the whole administration soon depended. Zachary Macaulay, father of the historian, had been made a passionate Abolitionist by time spent as the manager of a plantation in Jamaica. It was his greatest chance to do something for the Negroes, and he seized it with courage.

Macaulay soon had need of all his resolution, for shortly after the outbreak of war with France there was a major disaster. The little colony was attacked by a French squadron, piloted by an American slaver-captain. No resistance was offered, but the town was pillaged by Jacobin sailors, and some of the buildings burnt. Partly as a result of the setback, Macaulay's health broke down. After a short break at home, he resumed his post.

Soon the tide really turned. The French incursion had done good in restoring discipline. Building increased; agriculture and trade began to flourish. When Macaulay left, in the last year of the eighteenth century, he could claim that the colony was no longer an experiment, but established. It was recognised by the Government. The status of the original Company was raised, and it became the first of those Chartered bodies which were to take so great a part in the development of Africa. In 1808, Sierra Leone was given the government of a Crown Colony, its short history proof that intercourse between England and West Africa could rest on something finer than the Slave Trade. The independence of the country, in our own time, indicates how well the idealists built, how unanswerable their assertion that the Negro was 'a man and a brother'.

V

The hopes raised by the victory of the Nile came to nothing. Ireland became in rebellion, due largely to failure to admit Catholics to the Dublin legislature. The insurgents were indeed defeated at the well-named Vinegar Hill, and a French force, sent to their aid, landed at Killata only to be soundly beaten; but such encounters settled nothing fundamental.

On the Continent those spirits which had revived through Nelson's success were soon dashed. Bonaparte, eluding the sea-ward watch, escaped from Egypt. At the head of an experienced army, he then broke the Austrians at Marengo, while Moreau re-established French ascendancy in southern Germany.

At home, ever concerned with the country's strained finances and with the problem of meeting the enormous expenses of the war, Pitt introduced an income tax, amid a wail of protest. He levied ten per cent on incomes of £200 and upwards, with a lesser rate on those exceeding £60, and rich men told him that they faced ruin. His resignation from office, after he had united the Irish Parliament with that of the United Kingdom, was due to his inability to overcome George III's opposition to any wide measure of Catholic emancipation. If granted, this would, so the King indicated, once again cost him his reason.

'The King and Pitt part on affectionate terms,' wrote Wilberforce to Muncaster, 'the King saying that it is a struggle between duty and affection, in which duty carried it.' Pitt's astonishing tenure of office—eighteen unbroken years—was at last over.

In view of his country's peril, Pitt agreed to support Addington's administration, but he relaxed his own attendance in Parliament, and enjoyed some little leisure at Walmer, where he held the ancient office of Lord Warden of the Cinque Ports.

Addington was a strange choice as head of a great country, for he was a man of modest talents. These had been devoted, for some twelve years, to the Speakership, in which office he was liked for his pleasant manners and known for conservative habits of mind. A ditty ran that:

> *Pitt is to Addington*
> *What London is to Paddington*

—and it was true. Pitt apart, the ablest man in the House was Fox, but against him, even as a member of a Coalition, George III had a rooted prejudice, not perhaps unnatural, since Fox, on a public occasion had given the toast: 'Our Sovereign—the People', and had thereupon seen his name erased from the Privy Council. Until the brief Peace of Amiens, in reality a stalemate, with Britain predominant by sea and France by land, the Government was in the hands of mediocrities.

Addington was tepid, at best, on the Abolition question, and Wilberforce had to endure more disappointment. In 1798, and again the following year, he had proposed his regular motion for leave to introduce an anti-slave-trade Bill. He was supported on the first occasion by Fox, and on both by Pitt. 'I always have been', said the latter, 'and until my mind shall change its nature, I always shall be a friend to the immediate and unqualified abolition of the Slave Trade.' Windham, hitherto helpful, defected, but there was a recruit in Canning, whose fluent, witty speeches soon brought him to the front rank of the Commons.

Once more, it was defeat for the cause: in 1798 by 87 votes to 83, and in 1799 by 84 to 54. Wilberforce confessed to the House that the prospects for Abolition actually seemed weaker than they had when he had first raised the question, twelve years earlier. 'Hope deferred maketh the heart sick'—but not, it seemed, if that heart was Wilberforce's, and if his hopes were for others, not for himself.

So far was he from despair, that within a few weeks he was able to gain something in an unexpected direction.

He had discovered that an Order in Council existed which, in spite of the fact that Great Britain and Spain were at war, allowed trading to continue between the West Indian colonies of the two countries, slaves being the chief article of supply. The wretched Negroes were not, it appeared, safe from further peregrination even when they had survived the Middle Passage. They could be transferred, without let or hindrance, from the mercies of a British to that of a Spanish master.

An Order in Council was a matter in which Pitt could act. After some pressure on the part of Wilberforce, he had it rescinded, much to the planters' indignation. Wilberforce was not so successful with a Bill designed to protect the West African coast in the neighbourhood of Sierra Leone from the ravages of the traders. The second reading was carried by a tiny House, and it was then introduced to the Lords by Grenville. Thurlow, full of venom, spoke in opposition and he was supported by the Duke of Clarence. The Bill was rejected, and Sierra Leone remained in some danger. Thus far could lordly irresponsibility go in a matter which need affect no vital interests.

In 1802 Wilberforce told the House that he had not grown cold to the cause, and that at a future date he would once more ask their reconsideration of the slavery question. Two years later, when Pitt was again at the helm, called back by the reopening of war and the necessity of finding a man capable of facing Napoleon, he did so.

4   VICTORY

'How can I expect he should love me much', wrote Wilberforce of Pitt, 'who have been so long rendering myself in various ways vexatious to him?' In a sense he was right to ask the question, for Pitt, besides conducting a war against an enemy whose Grand Army was now massed against England on the opposite shores of the Channel, was in some difficulty with Parliament. In their way conditions were almost as trying as when he had first assumed supreme office, but now there was the handicap that he was many years older, and, though still only in his middle forties, in bad health. The King had refused him some of the men he wanted, and needed physicians in constant attendance, watching royal aberrations. Grenville and Windham, who had been refused office, had gone into opposition, their tongues bitter. Addington had been moved to the Lords, and Henry Dundas, now Viscount Melville and First Lord of the Admiralty, was his strongest political friend. Even he was under a cloud owing to rumours of a financial scandal of which more was likely to be heard.

Difficult as the times were, particularly for Pitt, they had grown more favourable for the cause of Abolition. Republicanism in France was dead, killed, as Burke had foretold, by a 'popular general's' sword. The nation was united as never before, not so much politically as by the danger which was visible on a clear day from the cliff-tops of the coast of Kent, and with danger, as so often, conscience revived. The effect of propaganda, if slow, was cumulative, and there was nothing to show on the other side. If Britain, as men believed, was engaged in a just war, how fitting that she should show the world an example of disinterested beneficence.

Under these auspices, the Abolition Committee, strengthened by the inclusion of Zachary Macaulay, by James Stephen, who had married Wilberforce's sister, and by Brougham, resumed activities. Pitt, still unable to pledge his Government, remained favourable, if no longer enthusiastic, and so it came about that on 30 May 1804 the familiar little figure once more rose from his place to ask the Common's leave to introduce an Abolition Bill. The House was fuller than usual, and the debate followed the lines of its predecessors.

Wilberforce outlined the case with clarity and moderation. Pitt welcomed new converts, and declared that, though the best kind of Abolition was total Abolition, yet he would support a gradual measure, if nothing else were obtainable. Fox held that the honour of the country was at stake. It was, so he said, being 'whispered through Europe that, however we might like lessons of morality, we could not be prevailed upon to give up a profitable branch of commerce'.

The most striking incident was the intervention of Irish Members. They had held a great dinner, more than thirty attending, at which their leader, Lord De Blaquiere, had proposed Wilberforce's health. They had no local interests connected with the Slave Trade, and were eager to assert their humanity. In a House of 173, no fewer than 124 voted for the motion, only 49 being against.

Congratulations poured in upon Wilberforce, but time had taught him to be wary. Twice before the House had voted the same way, but, in all the years, nothing had come of it. On the more cheerful side, earlier majorities had been small, and not to be depended upon. Now things were different, though there still remained the grimmest obstacle. 'I fear the House of Lords', said Wilberforce to the aged Newton, and he had long experience to daunt him. He was right in his foreboding. The Lords adjourned the Bill, by agreement, until the next session: obstruction, it seemed, would always find a way.

II

The year 1805 was crowded with events both glorious and sad. It saw the eclipse of Dundas; the victory of Trafalgar and the death of Nelson; the abandonment by the French of their plan of invasion; Napoleon's triumph at Austerlitz; the beginning of Pitt's fatal illness. Some of these events were connected. All had a bearing on the course of Wilberforce's life, and the first of them brought the last and darkest cloud between him and his old friend.

It may appear strange that in an age in which corruption was wide-spread, when 'interest' was as important to a man's career as either merit or principle, when boroughs were bought and sold, and when the Government was known to have effected the Union of British and Irish Parliaments largely by bribery, a matter of malversation of Admiralty funds, not by Dundas himself, but by an official in his department, the Deputy Treasurer of the Navy, should have led to such commotion. The sum in question, £10,000, had been used for private speculation, but it had resulted in no public loss. The underlying fact was that it provided a chance for enemies to get at Pitt through a man he had trusted. It was seized with both hands.

When the matter came before the Commons, debate was long and bitter. The removal of Dundas himself to the Lords gave opportunity for plain speaking, and the spectacle of Pitt at bay roused the hunting instincts of country gentlemen not always susceptible to the finer shades of loyalty. The going was hard throughout, and when, in the early hours of the morning, Wilberforce rose from one of the seats above the Treasury bench, it was noted that Pitt leant forward with an appealing glance. *Et tu, Brute*—so he must have felt: and as Wilberforce himself said: 'It required no little effort to resist the fascination of that penetrating eye.'

The appeal was too late. Wilberforce could not resume his seat, and he had already judged the case in the only possible way. Pitt knew that, in any matter of conscience, Wilberforce would speak according to principle:

> Here is a plain, broad fact which no subsequent elucidation can possibly explain away. Here is Lord Melville publicly declaring on his oath that

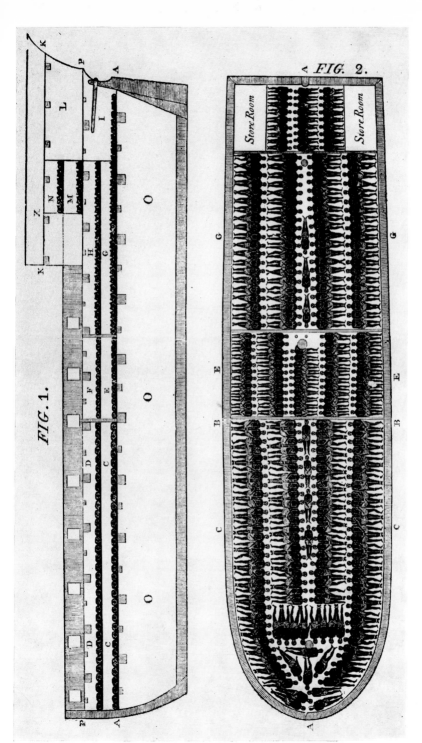

10   SECTIONAL VIEW OF SLAVER, USED BY WILBERFORCE IN HIS CAMPAIGN

11   EFFIGY OF WILBERFORCE IN HIS STUDY, AT HULL, WITH A PAINTING OF A SLAVE
BY BARKER OF BATH

he has tolerated his department in a gross breach of an Act of Parliament for the purposes of private emolument. . . . If the House were once to suffer a minister to say that he had connived at a breach of the law by a person who had been his confidential servant for a number of years, and that suspicion was to pass uncensored because no personal corruption had been proved against him . . . it would open a door to every species of corruption, and there would be no security left for the faithful discharge of any public trust.

This was true enough, and Wilberforce, with his known sincerity, had a great effect on the House. He was saying not only that right must be done, but that it must be seen to be done. Even so, Pitt's effort to have the Melville business referred to a Select Committee nearly succeeded. It was lost by the casting vote of the Speaker. Abbot, the man concerned, went 'as white as a sheet', so a witness said, and for two whole minutes sat still. Then, after a few words of explanation, he voted against Pitt. For once, as the opposition bawled 'Resign . . . *Resign* . . .' interspersed with 'View holloa. . . . We have killed the fox!', the man upon whom the burden of war was falling sat still in his place, his little cocked hat pressed down over his forehead to hide his tears.

Presently, with a bodyguard of the faithful to screen him from prying eyes, he was helped out of the House, dead beat. It was not so much that a personal friend had suffered, for Pitt and Melville were by then scarcely on speaking terms, but Pitt felt that his honour was engaged, and the defeat of the measure he proposed was a wound in his heart.

Melville resigned, and in the following year he was impeached in the House of Lords. He was acquitted on all counts—a verdict which might have been expected from the nature of the tribunal. But the earlier vote in the Commons had made it impossible for him ever to serve as a Minister of the Crown. 'I believe', wrote a Yorkshire voter to Wilberforce, 'that the delinquency of Lord Melville and the desertion of some of his oldest friends inflicted a wound upon Pitt's mind from which it never recovered.' Wilberforce wrote across the letter: 'It did not injure Pitt's health'—and for once, the comment seems both mistaken and self-justifying.

The resignation of the First Lord might have been serious for the conduct of the war at sea. Fortunately, Pitt could rely on the services of old Sir Charles Middleton, Wilberforce's friend and—with his late wife—an ardent Abolitionist. Middleton was nearly eighty, but he was raised to the peerage as Lord Barham, and it was he who, with masterly skill and unequalled experience in sea affairs, held strategical control in London during the campaign of Trafalgar.

That battle was fought and won in October, at the cost of Nelson's life ('so overcome', noted Wilberforce, and his feeling was universal, 'that I could not go on reading for tears'), and then, having turned his back upon the Channel shores, Napoleon continued the land campaign which led to victory at Ulm and Austerlitz. French successes, on so large a scale, saddened the last hours of William Pitt. The Minister, great in everything but in his attitude to religion, or so Wilberforce held, died on 23 January 1806, 'killed by the enemy as much as Nelson'. His last recorded words were a cry: 'Oh! my country! How I leave my country!'

> He left her [wrote G. M. Trevelyan, in a noble passage] in desperate straits, amid the ruins of those dynastic alliances by which he had three times striven in vain to make head against the French nation. He left her shorn of her ancient freedom of speech and thought, and that harmony of classes that had once distinguished 'merry England'. He had left her with her foot on Ireland prostrate and chained. But he left her recovered from the dishonour and weakness in which he had found her a quarter of a century before. He left her with Canada and India so established that they would not go the way of the lost Colonies. He left her able and willing to defy the conqueror of Europe when all others bowed beneath the yoke. He left her victor at sea, freshly crowned with laurels that have proved immortal. And if, in the coming era, Englishmen were divided class from class by new and bitter griefs, they had also a new bond of fraternity in the sound of Nelson's name.[1]

No statesman has had a juster epitaph. It was one which Wilberforce would have echoed.

His own place, as of right, was in the forefront of the funeral in Westminster Abbey. There, at the family's request, he carried the banner before Pitt's coffin. When, in that solemn hour, he stood beside it, it seemed to Wilberforce that the statue of Chatham 'looked down with consternation into the grave which was opened for his favourite son'.

[1] G. M. Trevelyan, *British History in the Nineteenth Century*, 1922 (p. 114).

III

Paradoxically, the death of Pitt helped the progress of Abolition, for the debates on the subject in 1805, the last in which he had taken part, went strangely. The first eight speakers, with one exception, were against the Bill, and even Fox was less vehement than usual. Pitt's own speech, which allowed his opinion to be inferred, was concerned mainly with the repudiation of a charge which an earlier speaker had made, that the Government had itself made an official contract for the purchase of slaves. He added that he had not risen 'with any intention of entering into the debate', and the already fallen spirits of enthusiasts sank to freezing-point. In all the years of their campaigning, Pitt had never, until now, failed to intervene.

When Wilberforce wound up, he made the only good speech of the day. He would be mad, he said, to look for Emancipation as the instant sequel to Abolition, but he hoped that one day, not far removed, slaves in the West Indies would be transformed into a free, moral and industrious peasantry. He added that if Parliament did nothing for the Negroes, it must be expected that sooner or later they would do what they could for themselves.

Seventy members voted for a second reading: seventy-seven were against it. As Wilberforce came away from the division, Mr. Hatsell, an experienced observer who had once been Clerk of the House, ventured to express his sympathy. 'Mr. Wilberforce,' he said, 'you ought not to expect to *carry* a measure of this kind. . . . You and I have seen enough of life to know that people are not induced to act upon what effects their interests by any abstract arguments.' 'Mr. Hatsell,' Wilberforce replied, 'I *do* expect to carry it; and what is more, I feel assured I shall carry it speedily.'

Privately, his thoughts were different: he was nearer despair than he had ever come before. The Irsh Members had either been absent, or had been got at by the planters. Even the Scots, usually so staunch, had in some cases turned their coats.

> I never felt so much on any Parliamentary occasion [Wilberforce wrote to Muncaster]. From the fatal moment of our defeat, I have had a damp struck into my heart. I could not sleep without dreaming of depredation

and cruelty on the injured slaves of Africa. . . . I really have no spirit
to write to you. . . . Still I will do all I can. If we cannot stop the whole
of this accursed traffic, it is much to stop half of it; and I am resolved to
do what I can, I repeat it.

There *was* in fact something he could do, as on the occasion of the
rescinding of the Order-in-Council permitting trade in slaves with
the Spaniards. Britain had recently annexed certain Dutch colonies,
Holland then being allied with France. Among them was Guiana.
Pitt had told Wilberforce privately that a trade in Negroes between
Africa and Guiana could be stopped by Proclamation, and he had
strongly opposed the subject being raised in the Commons. Satisfied
by this assurance, Wilberforce held his tongue, but for weeks,
nothing happened. Wilberforce pressed. Pitt delayed. It was, so
Wilberforce felt, inexplicable, and now that the motion for the
Abolition Bill had been lost he began to suspect, and he was not
alone in doing so, that Pitt had sold his conscience to retain the favour
of members of his Government. 'I write and call again and again',
he noted forlornly—but still nothing happened. 'Procrastination',
he told Muncaster, 'in one whom you used to call "The General"
has increased to such a degree as to have become absolutely
predominant.'

Exasperated as he was, Wilberforce made too little allowance for
Pitt's difficulties; pressure of work; the war; the increasing strain
on his health. But at last, patience was rewarded, and an appropriate
Order-in-Council issued. Wilberforce could not, alas, ascribe its
issue to reawakened conscience on the part of Pitt. It was due to the
business-like methods of Castlereagh, an anti-Abolitionist!

After Pitt's death, there was a necessary change of Government.
Grenville, on whom Wilberforce had come to depend even in the
Lords, was given the succession, and his Ministry, known as that
of 'All-the-Talents' included Fox, whom the King was at last
compelled to accept. With Windham and Addington, now Lord
Sidmouth, in office, Abolition could not even now be put forward
as a Government measure, but its chances were good, particularly
as Clarkson, whose health, which had once appeared to be broken,
had unexpectedly recovered. Clarkson set off like a giant refreshed
on a new tour of propaganda. What most heartened him, so he
found, was that the younger generation, who had grown up during

years of abeyance, embraced the cause with all the fervour that their elders had once displayed. Public opinion and political opportunity seemed at last to coincide.

Fox in office was a new man, though he was ageing. 'Quite rampant', so Wilberforce described him, 'and playful as he was twenty-two years ago, when not under awe of his opponents. . . . Talked as if we might certainly carry our question in the House of Commons, but should certainly lose it in the House of Lords.'

The first move was a Bill to prohibit the importation of slaves by British ships into Colonies annexed by Britain during the war, or into any Colonies of a foreign State, and to prohibit the outfitting of foreign slave ships in British ports, or the employment of British capital or labour therein. This was carried—even in the Lords, where the usual diatribes of the Duke of Clarence were answered by his royal cousin of Gloucester, who in a maiden speech condemned 'a shocking traffic in human blood'.

Fox had made it clear, and so did Grenville, that this Foreign Slave Bill would soon be followed by another, and that it was total Abolition they meant to have. 'The passing of it', said Fox, 'however unfortunate this Administration might be in other respects, would bestow more true glory upon it, and more honour upon our country, than any other transaction on which we could be engaged.' It was agreed that a motion for total Abolition should at once be prepared in both Houses.

On 10 June 1806, Fox in person moved the resolution, and in terms which lifted it high above party:

> So fully am I impressed with the vast importance and necessity of attaining what will be the object of my motion this day that, if during the almost forty years that I have now had the honour of a seat in Parliament, I had been so fortunate as to accomplish that and that only, I should think I had done enough, and could retire from public life with comfort and the conscious satisfaction that I had done my duty.

The resolution was supported by Romilly, the Solicitor-General, by Lord Henry Petty, Canning, and Wilberforce. It was opposed by Windham, Castlereagh, and Nelson's old friend Rose. The result was decisive: 114 votes to 15. Moreover, it was carried in the Lords, Sidmouth, Hawkesbury and Westmoreland being the only speakers in opposition. The walls of Jericho had fallen.

'If it please God to spare the health of Fox', said Wilberforce, 'and to keep him and Grenville together, I hope we shall see next year a termination of all our labours.' And with Fox's help, in that rewarding session, there was even time to rush a Bill through both Houses to prohibit the employment in the Slave Trade of any ships not hitherto engaged therein. At last—at long, long last, the enemy were on the run. Wilberforce would keep them at it.

IV

It is true that the last lap of a race is often the hardest, and it might well have been so in this case, for Fox was dying of dropsy. 'I quite love Fox', said Wilberforce (as well he might), 'for his generous and warm fidelity to the Slave Trade cause.' But alas, it was as with Pitt: 'he has not one religious friend, or one who knows anything about it'. Wilberforce was at Lyme Regis when he heard the news of Fox's death—and that of Thurlow. 'How speedily he has followed his great rival', he said. 'There is something which comes home to a man in the gradual quitting of the stage of those who are parts of the same *dramatis personae* as himself. I seem to be reminded that I am verging towards the close of the piece.'

It was not so. Wilberforce had nearly thirty years of life and activity before him, and he was now preparing his second book. It had begun as a pamphlet. It blossomed into a volume of nearly four hundred pages, for Wilberforce, like Parliamentarians of his time, was not often succinct. With the issue of *A Letter on the Abolition of the Slave Trade Addressed to the Freeholders and other Inhabitants of Yorkshire*, the final moves began.

The whirligigs of time were extraordinary, for Grenville, after consultations with Wilberforce, had decided to *start* matters in the very place where it had so often foundered before—the Upper House—and to make it the first important business of the new session.

Parliament met on 15 December, and on 2 January 1807, on the Prime Minister's motion, 'A Bill for the Abolition of the Slave

Trade' was read for a first time. A simple measure was put forward. The first clause provided that, after 1 May, the African Slave Trade and 'all manner of dealing and trading' in the purchase of slaves in Africa or their transport from Africa to the West Indies or 'any other island, country, territory or place whatever' is 'utterly abolished, prohibited and declared to be unlawful'. The second declared that any British ship thereafter employed in the Trade should be forfeited to the Crown. Further clauses provided for the penalisation of insurance contracts for safeguarding the Trade; for the payment of bounties for all slaves captured in British ships to the officers and men engaged therein, and for the placing of such captured slaves at the disposal of the Crown either for service in the Army or Navy, or for a limited and regulated apprenticeship to private persons.

Clarence, Westmoreland and Hawkesbury managed to delay matters for a month, but they could do no more, and when Grenville opened the debate on 5 February he paid a tribute which found an echo throughout Great Britain:

> The Bill will be supported in another place by a person to whom the country is deeply indebted for having originally proposed the measure, and for having followed up that proposition by every exertion from which a chance could be derived of success. I cannot conceive any consciousness being more truly gratifying than must be enjoyed by that person on finding a measure to which he has devoted the labour of his life carried into effect—a measure so truly benevolent, so admirably conducive to the virtuous prosperity of this country and the welfare of mankind—a measure which will diffuse happiness amongst millions now in existence, and for which his memory will be blessed by millions yet unborn.

Sidmouth, who spoke on the other side, preferred a 'rising tax on slaves'. Plain opponents included the unrepentant Duke of Clarence, Hawkesbury, St. Vincent (the great admiral's heart being with the mercantile marine), and Eldon, a formidable lawyer. Morton and Westmoreland brought the total to seven. Ten, including Grenville, spoke for Abolition—the Duke of Gloucester, once more a counterweight to the egregious Clarence, the Bishop of Durham, Selkirk, Rosslyn, King, Northesk (a counter to St. Vincent, for he had been third in command at Trafalgar), Moira, Holland and Suffolk. The reading was carried by a majority of 64. The final stages brought two more supporters in the Duke of Norfolk and the Bishop of London.

> Several peers [so Wilberforce noted in his diary] now speak with quite new civility. . . . How striking to observe Pitt and Fox both dead before Abolition effected, and now Lord Grenville, without any particular defence from Court, carries it so triumphantly. But let us not be too sure.

Grey, at that time Lord Howick, and one day to be 'Earl Grey of the Reform Bill' moved the reading in the Commons. He was Foreign Secretary, and was the appropriate Minister to do so, for this was a measure actually sponsored by the Government, even though it was not unanimous in its favour.

The crucial day was 23 February, and it was clear from the outset that it was to be an occasion, a 'great night', for the House showed signs of mounting excitement. Only one or two stalwarts cared to speak in opposition. Windham was silent—so were Rose and Castlereagh. Enthusiasm reached its height at the close of the speech by Romilly, the Solicitor-General, and its peroration was remarkable:

> When I look to the man at the head of the French . . . surrounded as he is with all the pomp and power and all the pride of victory, distributing Kingdoms to his family and Principalities to his followers, seeming when he sits upon his throne to have reached the summit of human ambition and the pinnacle of earthly happiness—and when I follow that man into his closet or to his bed, and consider the pangs with which his solitude must be tortured and his repose banished, by the recollection of the blood he has spilled and the oppressions he has committed—and when I compare those pangs of remorse with the feelings which must accompany my honourable friend from this House to his home, after the vote of this night shall have confirmed the object of his humane and unceasing labours; when he retires to the bosom of his happy and delighted family, when he lays himself down on his bed, reflecting on the innumerable voices that would be raised in every quarter of the world to bless him, how much more pure and perfect felicity he must enjoy, in the consciousness of having preserved so many millions of his fellow-creatures. . . .

Before he had finished, the storm broke. The House was on its feet, giving Wilberforce an ovation such as it had given to no living man. Round after round they cheered him. It was the most triumphant moment of his life, though he himself was scarcely conscious of it. In the midst of Romilly's tribute, when he spoke of his happy welcome home, Wilberforce's feelings overwhelmed him—he now had a nursery full of children. Insensible, as he afterwards confessed, to all that was passing, he sat bowed in his seat, his head in his hands, the tears streaming down his face.

Soon afterwards, the House divided. The second reading was carried by the tremendous majority of 283 to 16. On 25 March the King's assent was given, and the Bill became law.

12   A RUNAWAY SLAVE
From a nineteenth-century engraving

5   THE ELDER STATESMAN

WILBERFORCE's position was now unparalleled by any Commoner who had never been in office. He was not yet fifty, but he ranked in popular esteem with the great men of his age. It was no ignoble one, since it included Pitt, and Fox, and Burke, all, in their time, supporters of Abolition. His power for good was incalculable, his energy scarcely diminished. 'God will bless this country', he had written after his triumph, and he believed it. 'Well, Henry', he said gaily to Thornton, when the Clapham Sect assembled at Broomfield, to which house he had removed from Battersea Rise, 'what shall we abolish next?'

There was, indeed, still plenty for a man to do, even in Parliament. 'What greater enjoyment can there be in life', asked the Duke of Norfolk, 'than to stand a contested election for Yorkshire and win by one?' Wilberforce could have given him many answers, for, as he confessed to Muncaster, he 'sickened at a contest'. All the same. he would have to face one, for early in 1807 the Government decided on a dissolution. In the election which would follow, the rival candidates for Yorkshire, Lord Milton and Henry Lascelles, declared that they were prepared to spend recklessly in order to secure the two seats. Wilberforce, though well-to-do, was not immensely rich, and there was certainly a limit to what he would lay out, but how could he confess, by withdrawal, that he believed Yorkshiremen were bound to vote for money rather than for merit?

Milton stood for the Whigs, Lascelles for the Tories. Wilberforce, as an independent, had no resources of party behind him, while it was believed that his opponents would spend not less than £100,000 apiece. Yet independence was a quality which Yorkshiremen respect. 'We cannot desert Mr. Wilberforce', said a member of his audience on nomination day, and promptly put himself down for £500. Others took fire from his example. The sum of £18,000 was immediately subscribed, and money continued to flow in from every part of the county.

Transport was a difficulty. The other candidates had hired all the vehicles in the county, or so it seemed. 'No carriages are to be procured', wrote a supporter from Hull, 'but boats are proceeding up the river heavily laden with voters: farmers lend their waggons: even donkeys have the honour of carrying voters for Wilberforce; and hundreds are proceeding on foot.'

One such party was met by a member of Wilberforce's committee on the road from Wensleydale. He asked, 'For what parties, gentlemen, do you come?' The words with which he was greeted may still uplift the spirits of those with Yorkshire blood—'*Wilberforce to a man!*' they roared.

Ill organised as it was, such enthusiasm told. By the end of the fourth day of polling, Wilberforce was 111 ahead of Milton and 375 ahead of Lascelles. Every low trick was used by his opponents: lies; whispers; toughs and bullies who broke up meetings, so that it was sometimes impossible for Wilberforce to gain a hearing. On the twelfth day he fell ill, and could not leave his room. At once word went round that he was dead. The rumour was soon scotched, and in any case it did not matter, for at the final count the figures read— Wilberforce, 11,806; Milton, 11,177; Lascelles 10,989. No less than £70,000 had been subscribed on Wilberforce's behalf. More than half that sum was returned. Henry Lascelles must have had dour moments when he considered a six-figure outlay, all gone for nothing. As for Yorkshire, it took pride in having returned a man who had done good in the world—even if this had nothing to do with the county.

II

For the triumphant Member, there was much to be done, even now, in the African crusade. What had been settled was to make slave trading by British shipowners illegal—under penalties. But penalties, however severe, had never deterred smuggling. The area concerned was a long way off. Scarcity would raise prices. Temptation would press, perhaps for years. The next step should have been registration of all existing slaves, so that their number could not be added to without detection, but that was primarily a matter for the West Indian legislatures, and they, for their part, were disinclined to make any move in the matter. They had, so they considered, been slighted enough already.

It was true that the Royal Navy commanded the seas and would enforce the law, but the Navy could not be everywhere at all times, and it took long for the West African Negro to trust the sight of a British ship of any kind. This was instanced in the story told by the captain of a man-of-war. One day, H.M.S. *Assistance* was lying off the Guinea coast when a native came out in a canoe with fruit for sale. Finding the captain on the quarter-deck, the Negro asked: 'What ship?' 'King George ship' was the reply; 'Man-of-war ship.' But the Negro doubted. 'No,' he said, 'You Bristol ship.' Assurances were useless. The man became more and more alarmed. 'Dom your heart, you Bristol ship!' he cried at last. Leaping overboard and abandoning his canoe, he struck out desperately for the shore. His doubt was not unreasonable. Slavers, under one flag or another, were still about. Wilberforce was often at the Admiralty, asking for a 'sweep of the coast', or for more forces to be employed on anti-slavery patrols. Under conditions of the time, his requests could not always be met.

Then there were foreign Powers. Denmark was fulfilling her undertaking, and America approved Britain's lead, but France, Spain and Portugal were all in the business, and, as soon as circumstances permitted, they would doubtless resume it. When peace returned in Europe there would be much for Wilberforce to work for.

Meanwhile, he found it increasingly easy to support the war, now that Napoleon had shown so continuously that his objective was the domination of Europe—Britain included. When the Spaniards attempted to throw off the French yoke, Britain found in Wellington the military genius who would ensure them liberation. Once an army was established on Spanish soil, the country could at last begin to take the offensive, and pressure from the Iberian Peninsula, what Napoleon himself described as 'the Spanish ulcer', slowly began to force him into rasher and rasher enterprises. The Russian campaign of 1812, so bold and so disastrous; Wellington's successes; the Battle of the Nations, at Leipzig, where the Emperor was defeated, led to abdication—and to exile at Elba.

Issues nearer home which greatly concerned Wilberforce were, as of old, reform of the franchise, on which his views were moderately progressive, and Catholic Emancipation. 'Let us not be called upon to stand still,' he said, 'nor let us libel the Constitution so far as to say that it is necessary to its preservation that we should cherish its radical defects.' The Catholic question was at first bound up with Ireland, where Catholics could now vote, but could not sit in Parliament. This was anomalous, though not more so than many other circumstances of the time.

Wilberforce himself was possessed of such sturdy Protestant convictions that it was his hope that all his friends, and indeed the world at large, would in time come to share them. He spoke of 'our Protestant Empire'. As an Evangelical, tolerant of Dissenters—who had so staunchly supported his great cause—he was what would today be called Low Church. His ideas were far removed from Catholicism, which he feared, as did most Englishmen of his time, partly from historical memories, partly because of its unity and autocracy, partly from its power elsewhere.

There is little evidence to show whether Wilberforce ever studied with attention the basis of the Catholic claim that theirs was the one true Church, and he shared the view of many of his compatriots that Catholics, owing allegiance as they did to a Supreme Pontiff in another land, were a danger in his own. He also held to something more constructive than fear. It was his hope that Protestantism would gradually conquer even in Ireland; not by force but by persuasion. 'So long as the bulk of the Irish are Roman Catholics', he once told Grenville, 'the Protestants and the friends of Great Britain will be in truth a garrison in an enemy's country; and our great endeavour ought to be to enlighten and thereby, I trust, to convert the Roman Catholics. Much, I verily believe, might be done in that way in twenty or thirty years.' This may seem to have been an odd hope, considering that Wilberforce's knowledge of the world should have shown him that Protestantism, with its varieties in organisation—differing, for instance, even between England and Scotland—was a manifestation *local* in its application; but it was firmly held, and tenaciously kept. 'It is grievous to see', he said bitterly to Stephens after a Parliamentary debate, 'that we are only nominally a Protestant people.'

So keenly did he feel, that it would surely have saddened him that of his own four sons, William, Robert, Samuel and Henry— all of them devout men—no less than three, in the course of time, became Catholics. Even the elevation of Samuel to the Anglican sees of Oxford and Winchester successively would have consoled him only moderately, so careful had he been to try to form his boys in a school which he had found to answer his personal needs so well. It was a school which had produced Newton and Milner, and by the time of his elevation to a bishopric even Samuel had moved some way from their position, though he was too politic to be 'extreme' in his outlook.

Marianne Thornton, as so often, had views on the subject. When Henry Wilberforce went over to Rome, she said to Macaulay the historian that it would have surprised her less if 'Sam had been induced to believe in the winking Madonna and such nonsense'. 'Oh', said Tom Macaulay, 'if Bishop Sam had given up his bishopric there would have been no miracle in the matter, the Madonna would *really* have winked, I'm sure.'

III

It was the needs of his family, his sons and two daughters, which led Wilberforce to resign his seat as a Member for Yorkshire. 'My children, it is no exaggeration to declare, seldom get a quiet minute with me during the sitting of Parliament' he wrote, and he was never so happy as when in their company. He liked to read aloud to them on Sundays, and made them read to him, and when he could snatch an hour or two away from weekday business, he would take them off to an aquarium, or to the toy shops, or 'to see some jugglers'. He loved races and games, and had the gift of being able to blend the amusing and the serious. 'Mr. Wilberforce made us all very happy', wrote a friend after joining in a family party. 'He read, and talked, and carved, and reminded us of the benevolence of God.'

Not all meals were quite like that, particularly the breakfasts to which the eminent so often came, where guests helped themselves. Marianne Thornton remembered Wilberforce as 'so short-sighted he could see nothing beyond his own plate', which was always plied by a devoted wife, and she recalls that one day Isaac Milner, down from Carlisle and accustomed to open-handed ways, got so little that 'the Dean's stentorian voice was heard roaring out that there was nothing to eat, and desiring the servants to bring bread and butter. He added "and bring plenty, without limit!" Wilberforce meanwhile joined in with "Thank you, thank you kindly Milner, for seeing to these things. Mrs. Wilberforce is not strong enough to meddle much in domestic matters."'

Before resigning his seat, Wilberforce consulted earnestly with friends. Henry Thornton was against it; so was the Speaker, when asked for his official view. James Stephen suggested a seat with little or no local obligations. Babington thought complete retirement the best answer. But after having enjoyed, as well as suffered, the hurly-burly of more than thirty years of Parliamentary life, Wilberforce could not bring himself to forgo politics completely, and it was Stephen who carried the day. He often did.

The two men had become neighbours in Kensington, in houses with gardens, a particular boon to Wilberforce, who loved flowers almost as much as children. Stephen was now his closest friend, one with whom he rarely disagreed.

The matter once decided, the rest was simple. Mrs. Wilberforce's cousin, Lord Calthorpe, had exactly the thing. It was the pocket borough of Bramber, an out-of-the-world village near the Sussex coast. There would be no scramble for representation, no outlay— Lord Calthorpe would gladly give the place in Parliament to his celebrated kinsman: and so it was. Mrs. Wilberforce remarked upon it as one of the better compensations of an unreformed House of Commons. Lord Calthorpe asked Wilberforce 'in the kindest manner possible . . . to consider it quite as my own': and it was as Member for Bramber that he continued his Parliamentary life, eased of much of its burdens.

In the autumn of 1812 Wilberforce published a 'resigning advertisement' in the Northern Press. When it appeared, a meeting of electors passed a resolution of thanks for his 'unremitting and impartial attention to the private business of the county, and for his independent and honest performance of his trust on every public occasion':

> As freeholders of Yorkshire resident in or near Hull, we indulge in the grateful feelings of an honest pride; we exult in the reflection that the illustrious names of those incorruptible patriots Marvell and Wilberforce, adorn our records and shed a lustre on this, the place of their nativity.

Such tributes were pleasing because they were sincere and true. Another, equally warming in a different way, came from the unregenerate Sheridan. Meeting him in the street one day, Sheridan said that when he heard that Wilberforce was giving up his seat for Yorkshire, he had been tempted to write to urge him to reconsider the matter. 'Though you and I have not much agreed in our votes,' he said, 'yet I thought the independent part you acted would render your retirement from Parliament a public loss.'

Sheridan was right, for although acceptance of the Bramber seat meant that Wilberforce could give more attention not only to his family but to other interests such as the British and Foreign Bible Society, the Church Missionary Society (through which the earnest hoped to influence religious beliefs held in the East) and the African Institution, which was to be the heir of the Abolition Committee and to some degree of the older Sierra Leone Company, there was much official business still to engage him.

So far as the Slave Trade was concerned, an early shock came from Portugal. In conversations with representatives from that country, conducted through Castlereagh, it was soon evident that the Portuguese were trying to drive a bargain—'audacious and even atrocious' Wilberforce rightly called it—which would guarantee Portugal uncontrolled extension of the Slave Trade south of Cape Palmas, if she abstained from operating north of it.

13 SLAVES ON A QUAY-SIDE
From a watercolour by
B. Reading

14 BRANDING A
WOMAN SLAVE
From a contemporary
engraving

My dear Lord Melville

Allow me to take the...

Lyme Oct. 27th 1804

...to Lieutenant Frederick Parker of the Leda —

Admiralty 24th Nov 1804

My dear Sir,

I have received your letter...

Your...
W Wilberforce

15 LETTER, HITHERTO UNPUBLISHED, FROM WILLIAM WILBERFORCE TO LORD MELVILLE, AND THE ANSWER

The subject of the letter, Lieutenant Parker, was promoted in 1806 by Lord Barham, Melville's successor as First Lord of the Admiralty

This was the first of a series of embarrassments into which the campaign for Abolition led the British Government, and it justified some of the cynicism with which opponents had conducted their case. For it was soon clear that many foreigners regarded the whole business as an instance of British meddling, and, no doubt, hypocrisy. There was, it was argued abroad, much more behind it than mere disinterested humanitarianism. It was a deep-laid plot to ruin the commercial interests of rival Powers. Severed from free intercourse with her neighbours as Britain had so long been, these same neighbours had had no opportunity to study such altruists as Wilberforce. It took time to become used to the phenomenon; meanwhile, there was fruitful cause for trouble and misunderstanding of every kind.

This was so chiefly with the Latin countries: northerners under-stood better—even the Tsar of Russia. 'I am about to correspond with a real live Emperor,' so Wilberforce told Gisborne, 'not merely such a sort of Birmingham emperor as Bonaparte.' But when (after Leipzig) Paris and later Vienna became the scene of negotiations, matters grew ever more difficult. 'Their merchants', wrote Wilber-force of France, 'are intent on gain anyhow . . . and all the old *amis des noir* are in exceedingly bad odour.'

Wellington, who opposed the Slave Trade on the simple ground of humanity, wrote to Wilberforce to describe the prejudice of all classes in France on the subject, particularly 'those of our determined enemies, the principal officers and employees'. He continued:

> I was . . . told gravely by the Directeur de la Marine that one of our objects in abolishing the slave trade was to get recruits to fight our battles in America . . . and it was hinted that a man might as well be a slave for agricultural labour as a soldier for life, and that the difference was not worth the trouble of discussing.

'Our battles in America' referred to the short but bitter war, chiefly over the right of search at sea, in which Britain and America had been engaged; and there were other Frenchmen beside M. le Directeur who considered that the life of a slave in the West Indies was not as intolerable as idealists would maintain.

In the summer of 1814, the Tsar Alexander came to London and asked to see Wilberforce. 'Got up by half-past six', noted the diary,

'that I might pray God for a blessing on my interview.' Alexander
was affable and sympathetic. But he pointed out that it was lack
of British insistence that had prevented Abolition from being
written into a European settlement. This was a signal for Wilberforce
to mobilise public opinion once more on the slave's behalf. Castlereagh, who would conduct future negotiations, was aware of the
strength of public feeling in England, but he soon came up against
a point of national honour in the case of France. That country would,
so she declared, never be dictated to in such a matter as Abolition.
Fortunately the newly restored Bourbon, Louis XVIII, was an
ardent partisan—he was said to have been the only genuine one in
France; and there was always Wellington.

The first success was unexpected. An ordinance was published
forbidding French subjects to engage in the Slave Trade north of
the mouth of the Niger. The Guinea Coast, it seemed, was to be
spared a revisitation of French slavers—if, that is, the ordinance
was to be more than a gesture. '*C'est vous et Lord Wellington*', wrote
Madame de Staël to Wilberforce, '*qui aurez gagné cette grande
bataille pour l'humanité.*'

Then, amid Congresses and discussions among his enemies,
Napoleon escaped from Elba. On 1 March 1815 he landed at Cannes.
Less than three weeks later, he was back at the Tuileries. Preparing at
once for battle, he first spoke fair words: he informed the Allied
Sovereigns, then at Vienna, that it was his dearest wish 'to make the
Imperial Throne of France a bulwark for the Peace of Europe'. As
for England, he had a master-stroke. With complete understanding
of what was likely to bedevil Anglo-French relations, he boldly
bid for the favour of the British Government and people by
proclaiming the immediate and total Abolition of the Slave Trade.
A Bourbon ordinance, limited in its scope, was one thing—his own
decision, clear and unequivocal, was quite another.

After Napoleon's Hundred Days of renewed power were over,
after Wellington and Blücher had, at Waterloo, decided the future
of Europe—Blücher actually sending word from the field of battle
to Wilberforce—after the trembling Louis XVIII was back on the
throne, it was impossible for the most stubborn French reactionary
to contrive a reversal of Napoleon's edict, in direct antagonism to
England.

I have the gratification of acquainting you [wrote Castlereagh to Wilberforce in July 1815] that the long desired object is accomplished, and that the present messenger carries to Lord Liverpool the unqualified and total Abolition of the Slave Trade throughout the Dominions of France.

In his own way, Wilberforce was as complimented at the general Peace as his friendly helper, Wellington. The Tsar continued to be personally interested in the slaving question; the Duchess of Oldenburg insisted on an interview with the Abolitionist; the King of Prussia gave Wilberforce a set of china—'the only thing I ever got by spouting', as the recipient smilingly said: but what touched him more than any of these things was that when he went for a holiday in a Devon village, the moment it was known he had arrived, ringers went to the church tower and greeted him with a peel of bells.

IV

For the mass of people, peace was to prove as hard as war—for the poorest, harder. In 1814 the price of corn fell heavily, and the resulting boon to the townsman seemed to show that, with Napoleon in exile, they might hope for something better than to be constantly on the edge of starvation. But ships from abroad, bringing in their cargoes of grain to sell in a ready market, meant disaster to home agriculture, geared as it had been in war-time to the growing of corn. Farmers gave up in despair: landlords, with derelict acres on their hands and mortgages which soon became crippling burdens, saw their dream of permanent war prices and high rents dissolve. Something, they decided, must be done at once.

The speed of legislation proved not only that agriculture was the largest industry of the country, but that the Houses of Parliament, full as they were with the 'landed interest', would ensure, for decades to come, that land was first, the towns a long way second. In the spring of 1815, a Corn Law was passed forbidding the importation of corn unless the price of wheat stood at more than eighty shillings a quarter. Such a hasty measure may for the time have saved agriculture, but it brought instant distress to the towns, and this was to endure for more than thirty years. It also increased pressure for Parliamentary reform, if only to adjust the balance between urban and rural representation.

'Public discontent running high, Corn Bill *causa*', noted Wilberforce in March; and a little later: 'Corn Bill in Committee—sad rioting at night. Both doors of the carriage which set Members down opened, and Members pulled out. None much injured.' The Cockney knew little of economics, but that little was enough to tell him that he would get the worst of any current legislation.

'People savage and inveterate . . . Charles Grant and Mr. Arthur Young . . . slept with us for security', noted Wilberforce. Another personality marked out for abuse was Sir Joseph Banks, President of the Royal Society, who, with Arthur Young, had in fact done much for the improvement of agriculture.

For some time, Wilberforce debated whether he should speak on the question in Parliament. His personal interests were not involved. He was never a landed proprietor, and he could afford to buy his bread at any ruling price. All the more reason, he decided, to speak from his inner convictions, and so he did. He said:

> There was a general impression that the opening of our ports freely for the importation of foreign corn would prevent agriculturalists from supplying our home market and would occasion a general decline and decrease of our agriculture. If that were true, it was necessary for the general weal of the Empire that the Legislature should adopt proper remedies before it was too late. . . . It was worthy of the most serious consideration that those very countries from which we might derive supplies were countries which, at no great length of time, might be united against this nation. . . . No, there could not be any truth more certain than this—that a great country like England should be in- dependent of foreign nations with regard to the supply of food. Manufacturers were protected: why not agriculture too, to save workers on the land. . . . As to the cost of bread, he had not heard one single argument to show that, because the restricting price was fixed at 80 shillings, the price of corn must necessarily be raised to that extent. At the same time he was personally in favour of the lower limit of 76 shillings.

As a result of his views, he became the object of hostile attention. Early next day one of his former servants, who had set up as a greengrocer, went as usual to Covent Garden for his supplies. 'So your old master has spoken for the Corn Bill', he was told. 'His house shall pay for it.' The threat came to nothing, but it was taken seriously, and a sergeant, four soldiers, and a 'peace officer' were stationed to protect him. 'Were you to enter the dining-room at family prayer time,' he wrote to a friend, 'you would probably think we were expecting a visit from the ex-Emperor.' A few days later he noted in his diary: 'The soldiers (Scotch) behave extremely well; they come in to prayers, and are pleased to do so.'

The virtues of political independence were considerable and obvious, but when, as in the case of Wilberforce, they seemed so often to agree with measures of repressive Governments, they were bound to be misunderstood—hence the dislike he aroused in such forthright Radicals as Cobbett, and in such mordant spirits as William Hazlitt who, in the *Spirit of the Age*, called him 'as fine a specimen of *moral equivocation* as can well be conceived'.

Even in the Commons, the Opposition objected at least once to Wilberforce sitting in their side of the House, and George Tierney, their leader said—more good humouredly than print may convey if Wilberforce was right in what he noted in his diary:

> I do not wish to speak disrespectfully of the honourable Member for Bramber; and certainly there is no individual more capable of giving effective support to Ministers and their measures when he chooses to turn out (*cheers and laughter*). What his vote will be on the present occasion it is not, perhaps, easy to prophesy. . . . Generally, his phraseology is happily adapted to suit either party; and if, now and then, he loses the balance of his argument and bends a little to one side, he quickly recovers himself and deviates as much in an opposite direction as will make a fair division of his speech on both sides of the question.

This glimpse of Wilberforce as Bunyan's Mr. Facing-both-ways was unfair, but it had enough element of truth to cause laughter. It was, however, not unkindly. 'Wished not to speak', noted Wilberforce. 'Tierney gave me the last prick which forced me to rise; though not at all ill-naturedly, I am glad to say. Nor was I ill-natured, I hope. Thank God, I did not feel so.'

It was impossible to be vexed for long with such a man, though it was a common criticism that the zealot who had done so much for the Negro, who had such general influence, did so little, or so it seemed, except in the way of private charity, for the oppressed at home. There, always, he was on the side of law and order, of the establishment, of improvement by gradual stages, of acceptance of rank and station on the Wesleyan pattern.

Such an attitude was bound to be comforting to those in power, since he spoke for many, but it did not generate enthusiasm in those who hoped to find in him a champion of advanced opinion. And as he grew older, Wilberforce's interests became increasingly diffused —except on the slavery question—while his power to raise public opinion, always considerable, was used with caution.

The fact was that it appeared to him, as to others of his class and generation, that, if the old Jacobinism was dead, something almost as dangerous was replacing it. This was so—and for the sufficient reason that, for a great number, for most of the time, conditions of life were almost intolerable. The Industrial Revolution was, with every year, gathering momentum, and the country was not ready— would not be ready for decades, to deal wisely with its consequences. It was bringing prosperity, but at first for the few. In business, the principle of *laissez-faire* was sacred, and *laissez-faire* meant that the master drove the hardest possible bargain with his men, with the law, and pressure of hunger, on his side.

Wilberforce drew his wealth from merchandising, and later from banking. He had no direct experience even of this, being content, sensibly enough, to allow his affairs to be looked after by others skilled in such matters. The owning and personal control of one small factory would have taught him much: and it is fair to think that he would have treated his work-people like a family, since he was never less than generous in his dealings with his fellow-men. Denied that enlightening experience, he spoke and acted as one who was too often content to let affairs of State be managed by others less scrupulous than himself.

V

With all this said, there was much—as Mr. Tierney would have mockingly put it—on the other side, and it was notable that when Wilberforce was moved to support acts of amelioration, it was because he had been convinced not so much by abstract argument as by concrete instances, by actual people and their distresses. It had been so with the Slave Trade; it was so with the savage Penal Code of the country—'our bloody laws' as he was once, at least, incited to call them.

'An affecting visit from Mrs. B.', he noted soon after the Corn Law riots, 'the wife of an attorney of respectable station and character, near thirty years in Leeds, convicted of forgery on stamps and deeds, and to be hanged this day week.' Two years later, he was consulted by Elizabeth Fry 'about a poor woman under sentence of death for forgery'—again he burst forth about 'our murderous laws'. In 1819 he presented a petition to the Commons on the subject from a number of Quakers, and in doing so lamented that he could 'write but little, and scarcely read at all'—he had been over-taxing his strength. But it was his voice which ensured a Committee to study the matter, and on this he served, the resulting recom-mendations procuring some mitigation of the graver penalties.

On the Game Laws he was prepared to express views unpopular with his friends. 'It is not considered any crime', he said, 'to purchase game for a gentleman's table, while the poor wretch who purloined it may suffer the loss of his liberty and perhaps be led to the gallows.' This was a reference to the fact that though it was in fact unlawful for anyone to buy or sell game, yet it was everywhere done, and at inflated prices, owing to the extreme hazard to the poacher. So ridiculous were the laws on the subject, that it was also illegal for anyone who was not a squire or a squire's eldest son to kill game, even at the invitation of the owner, an inconvenience which could be got round by a process known as 'deputation'.

In 1819 Wilberforce declared the Game Laws

> so opposite to every principle of personal liberty, so contrary to all our notions of private right, so injurious and so arbitrary in their operation that the sense of the greater part of mankind is in determined hostility to them.

The 'greater part of mankind' was one thing, the House of Commons was another. There, he spoke in a minority. He was no 'sportsman', in the technical sense of the term, while the House was full of eager pursuers of game. It was many years before Lord Althorp swept the older laws into limbo, almost unremarked, amid the turmoil of the Reform Bill.

For Elizabeth Fry's work among women prisoners Wilberforce had active sympathy. In February 1818 that pioneer, together with the Buxtons, Samuel Hoare and Priscilla Gurney, dined at Kensington. 'Very interesting talk', noted the host, 'and agreed to meet tomorrow at Newgate.' The visit to the most famous of all gaols impressed him. 'The order she has produced is wonderful', he said: 'much talk with the Governor and Chaplain—Mrs. Fry prayed in recitative—the place from its construction bad.' A few weeks later he added: 'What lessons are taught by Mrs. Fry's success! I am still warmed by the account. Were I young, I should instantly give notice of the business, if no one else did.'

The conditions of child labour in factories also moved his compassion, and he spoke on the subject whenever it was raised in the House. As for the chimney boys, a regulating Act of 1788, passed with great difficulty, had never been enforced. Masters still found it cheaper to drive children through soot-choked chimneys than to use long brushes. Not infrequently they were choked: sometimes they were burnt to death: always they suffered, not only in health and happiness, but through the humiliation of being permanently black.

Wilberforce thought much on the subject of the child sweeps, and with good reason, since they provided a notorious instance of humane legislation being disregarded, a practice which he had met with continuously in the sphere which he had made his own. It was so not only with the earliest Act affecting sweeping, but it went on. Succeeding Acts were rendered dead-letters by the callous connivance of private house-holders, local authorities and magistrates, and in 1875, long after Wilberforce had been gathered to his fathers, Lord Shaftesbury noted in his diary:

> One hundred and two years have elapsed since the good Jonas Hanway brought the brutal iniquity before the public, yet in many parts of England and Ireland it still prevails with the full knowledge and consent of all classes.

It needed Shaftesbury's persistence, and the impact of Kingsley's *Water Babies*, to kindle the public conscience enough to ensure that the bad old days at last ended. Legislation without enforcement was only one degree removed from no action at all, and the best insurance that a law would be enforced was pressure of public opinion.

VI

One day, Marianne Thornton saw Wilberforce holding a flower, commending its beauty: 'And oh!', he added, more to himself than to the company, 'how unlike the Queen's countenance!' He was referring to Queen Caroline, and that he should ever have been involved with her at all recalls one of the stranger incidents of his life.

George III died in 1820, by then both mad and blind, and his successor, who had shown a friendly and considerate side to Wilberforce ever since, as Prince of Wales, he had admired Wilberforce's singing, was in a dilemma owing to the conduct of his wife. Their marriage had never been felicitous, but having for some years lived an eccentric life abroad, Caroline was now determined to assert her rights as Queen of England. Her husband was equally resolved to refuse them, at the price, if need be, of instituting proceedings for divorce—this in spite of the notorious irregularity of his own way of living.

Lord Liverpool was then Prime Minister, and he and his Cabinet soon found themselves in a dilemma. They knew that if he insisted on his own way George IV would incur odium with the mass of his people, and his Ministers with him: they also knew that if he were thwarted, he was capable of dismissing his Government and, in his father's phrase, 'looking about him'.

A compromise was attempted. The Ministers agreed to the King's demand that Caroline's name should be omitted from the prayer for the Royal Family in the Liturgy on the understanding that the King should abandon attempts to prosecute his wife. But such an arrangement took Caroline herself out of account. It was by no means acceptable to her, and she promptly set out from Italy on her way to England, insistent that she should be recognised in every way, Prayer Book included. She was met at Montbard by her doughtiest champion, Alderman Wood, and at St. Omer by Brougham, whom she had chosen as her principal legal adviser. On 5 June she landed at Dover. Next day she drove through cheering crowds to London.

> She approaches wisely, because boldly [noted Wilberforce]. How deeply interested all are, indeed I feel it myself, about her. One can't help admiring her spirit, though I fear she has been very profligate.

Public opinion had turned to Wilberforce a few years earlier, when Mrs. Clarke, the mistress of the Duke of York, had been interrogated by a Committee of the House of Commons as being suspected of selling commissions in the Army. Wilberforce had then spoken out without fear of offending the royal family, and the Duke, very properly, had resigned. People now turned to him again, in a question where justice, morality, the dignity of the Crown, and the whole system of Government was involved. It was a moment for the most eminent of independents to give a lead.

Behind the King stood his somewhat reluctant Government, and the Tories of the right. Behind the Queen was Brougham, with his eloquence and his legal skill, together with most of the Whigs, and the vociferous people, who liked, after their fashion, to champion the abused.

Wilberforce's first proposal was for a pause on both sides, 'with the declaration that its purpose was to give the opportunity for a final settlement'. Conferences took place. The King made various concessions: the name and rights of Queen without reserve: a royal yacht: Caroline's rank to be notified to the Court of the country where she intended to reside, and an Address to be presented to thank Her Majesty for having acceded to the wishes of the House of Commons.

On the question of the Liturgy, George IV remained adamant, and he took no notice of a letter sent to him by Wilberforce praying for an act of grace in this matter, and warning him of the dangerous state of feelings in the country.

> I fear [ran an entry in the diary] lest it should please God to scourge the nation through the medium of this rupture between the King and Queen. If the soldiery should take up her cause, who knows what may happen—and is it very improbable? O Lord, deliver us.

His next effort, since the King was unyielding, was to try to get the Queen to agree to submit on this point. At first he had good hopes, indeed Brougham went so far as to pledge himself she would do so.

On that understanding, when Wilberforce and three other members of the Commons waited on Caroline with the Address, he found a mob at the door of Wood's house, where she was staying. 'If it had been night', said Wilberforce, it 'would have been very dangerous.' As it was, the Members were hissed and booed, though no stones were thrown. When they were received in audience, they found their mission a failure. Caroline had never trusted Brougham—'if my head is on Temple Bar', she said 'it will be his doing'—and she had been listening to other advice, including that of Wilberforce's arch-enemy Cobbett.

Cobbett told her, not untruly, that it was the general hope that she would refuse to yield on the question of the Liturgy, or indeed on any other. Later he wrote:

> Mr. Wilberforce's motion is clearly seen through by the public, who have no doubt that it is intended to effect by supplication that which is perceived cannot be effected by threats. . . . The writer of this paper presumes humbly to express an opinion that the Answer to this Address should *explicitly reject the advice* contained in it. . . . An Answer of this description would, it is believed, put a stop to the efforts of Mr. Wilberforce.

Wilberforce read the Address, and Caroline formally rejected it. 'Her manner', he said, 'was extremely dignified, but very stern and haughty.' Cobbett had won, and Wilberforce was angrily accused of having misled and humiliated the House of Commons, the King's partisans denouncing him as an irresponsible busybody. It was then that he showed what Brougham described as 'a political forbearance which I never knew equalled'. It would have been easy enough to clear himself by producing Brougham's written pledge that the Queen's attitude would be favourable. He did not do so. Brougham had helped him in the matter of the Slave Trade, and he never forgot kindnesses, political or otherwise.

Public washing of linen was now inevitable. Since Caroline had refused compromise, the King determined on a Bill of Pains and Penalties as an instrument of divorce. He would get rid of her in the manner of Henry VIII, though not, indeed, at the cost of her head—times had moved far enough from the Renaissance for that.

Despite the humiliation of the rejected Address, there were those who still hoped Wilberforce might prevent the worst. 'He is looked up to', wrote Madame d'Arblay, 'as the only man in the Dominions to whom an arbitration should belong.' An impulsive go-between even sent a messenger to fetch Wilberforce from Weymouth, where he was staying, to see the King, who was informed that he was expected. Wilberforce refused to set out on such a hasty errand, and

he was right, for George said that if he conferred with Mr. Wilberforce, it must be on some political business, and that he never talked
on political subjects except to his Ministers. Thereupon, what
became known as the 'Queen's Trial' proceeded on its course.

> It will be long, painful and disgusting [Wilberforce told the House],
> and what in my mind aggravates the evil, Parliament is not clear in the
> matter. We marry our Kings and Queens contrary to the laws of God
> and nature, and from this source proceed the evils I am now anxious to
> avoid.

Day after day the Queen sat in the crowded Chamber of the House
of Lords while the Crown Lawyers tried—with a procession of
wretched Italian witnesses—to prove her guilty of adultery. It was
an unhappy spectacle, food for the popular Press, but not edifying
for a leading country in Europe. Nor did the trial succeed: the Bill
passed the Lords with such slight and falling majorities that Ministers
at length abandoned it.

> This morning [noted Wilberforce in November 1820] the early coaches
> from London came in, men and horses covered with white favours—
> emblematic, I suppose, of her innocence—for the rejection of the Bill
> against the Queen or rather for Lord Liverpool's giving it up when
> carried only by nine.

Yet when it was all over, Caroline, nominally victorious, must
have wondered whether Cobbett had been right. 'No one in fact
care for me', she said pathetically, 'and dis business has been more
cared for as a political affair dan as de cause of a poor forlorn
woman. . . .' It was difficult to feel much for Caroline personally, so
acutely eccentric was she, and so averse, for all her occasional
dignity, from even such elementary measures of personal cleanliness
then usual in her state of society: all the same, her virtues included
courage, and when the King refused her the share she claimed in his
Coronation, she renewed her fight. The Privy Council had decided
against her claim: the Archbishop of Canterbury told her he could
only officiate by orders of the Sovereign—but on the day in
question Caroline drove to Westminster Abbey and asked to be
admitted.

It was her last gesture, and what broke her heart, as she was
turned away, was that the fickle crowd broke into laughter, crying
at her 'Shame' and 'Off!'. Within a fortnight, she was dead.

Wilberforce, not Cobbett, had been right. He had tried to blend chivalry with attention to the King's wishes, and had tried to end a public scandal before it had begun. It says much for the attachment of England for her monarchy that the institution could survive such episodes, and that the people enjoyed—and paid for—one of the most extravagant coronations in history. It was, said Wilberforce, 'the finest raree show ever exhibited. But the moral eye seems to have been too much distracted, and it wanted the solemn effect which the mind contemplates in a King with his nobles about him, taking oaths of fidelity to his people, and their emotions of loyalty towards him.'

VII

There were other issues raised, during his later years in Parliament, where Wilberforce was on what history shows to have been the right side. He remained consistent in his belief in at least some degree of reform in borough and franchise, and he spoke nobly, more than once, on the question of Catholic disabilities in Ireland.

England's treatment of Ireland, so he told the House in 1821, was 'enough to awaken every generous sympathy in the human mind'. He reminded Members that while the Glorious Revolution of 1688 had given England what she wanted—a Protestant Succession and a satisfactory measure of liberty—it had brought no corresponding comfort to Ireland, and he thought that, over the centuries, England had treated Ireland as a stepmother her stepchild. 'Can it be wondered at', he asked, 'that she has struggled to shake off the yoke of her oppressors?'

He was not alarmed by those who said that no Catholic would be satisfied with any concession short of a seat in Parliament. Would that be so great an evil? If Irish Catholics were hostile to this country, all the more reason for bringing them into the British legislature, where their prejudices would be softened by a closer knowledge of the country and its constitution. To give Catholics in Ireland the vote, and to go no further, was to let them out of prison and keep them in convict's dress. The measure which he was supporting passed the Commons—but was rejected in the Lords. So often did this happen in the case of enlightened proposals, that the nation's patience with the Upper House is as much to be wondered at as in that of some of its Kings. Ten years later, at the time of the Reform agitation, patience at last became exhausted, and it was not before time.

As might have been expected, in foreign affairs Wilberforce was invariably on the liberal side in an era marked by severe reaction. For instance at the time of the War of Greek Independence he spoke with the feelings common to everyone who had been nurtured on the Classics, and who had kept his learning alive:

> It is a disgrace to all the powers of Europe that, long ere now, they have not made a simultaneous effort and driven back a nation of barbarians, the inveterate enemies of Christianity and freedom, into Asia. . . . I know of no case in which the power of a mighty country like England could be more nobly, more generously, or more justifiably exerted than in rescuing the Greeks from bondage and destruction.

Reform—Ireland—Greece: these were among the more important matters which engaged Wilberforce's attention as a legislator: but his main interest remained the slaves. For them there was still, despite his hard-won success, almost everything to do.

6   SLAVES STILL IN CHAINS

THERE is distance between words and deeds, between laws and action, even in the best-intentioned countries. Sometimes this is bridged slowly, sometimes not at all. It was so with Abolition.

After the end of the long war in Europe, many sovereign rulers enacted that general Abolition of the Slave Trade should apply to territories under their sovereignty, but they did not always carry it out. With one exception, the Tsar of Russia, they or their subjects were not in earnest, and Russia was not a sea Power. Only Britain, with public opinion behind her rulers, and with an efficient Navy to implement their directions, meant what she said. Even in her case, the Colonies were in undisguised opposition.

Two Powers stood unregenerate: Spain and Portugal: the ancient rivals to Britain in the New World. They needed bribes to move in any way at all. In 1815 the Portuguese agreed—with a *douceur* from the British Treasury by way of compensation—to limit their share in the Trade to the West Coast of Africa south of the Equator, and made vague promises of total Abolition 'in the near future'.

Spain pleaded that, owing to the war, her Colonies were not so well stocked with slaves as the British West Indies had been in 1807; she made much of economic loss, and of the difficulty of compensating traders. She also protested that Britain had seized some of her slave ships, and had refused to restore them. A bargain was hinted at; and at the prospect of money, matters quickened:

With unfeigned joy I state to you [wrote Wilberforce to Stephen in 1816] that I have just heard from Lord Castlereagh that the Council of the Indies, to which the whole question of the Abolition had been referred by the Spanish Government, has reported in favour of total and immediate Abolition. But a majority of seven, of whom one has large property in Cuba, has protested against the others and made a separate report. Even they, however, have recommended Abolition north of the Line immediately, and totally in five years. But all the Council seems to wish to make it a condition that we should give them money or at least give up their captured ships.

In the following year Castlereagh—not personally an ardent convert to the crusade, but as Foreign Secretary doing his duty with a will—summoned Wilberforce to town. 'With him for about an hour', Wilberforce noted. 'He really takes much pains for the cause. He says he was written more on this head than on any other. The Spaniards are pressing hard for £600,000 and a loan.'

The basis for the treaty as drafted in 1817 for signature by Spain was that Spain undertook to abolish the Trade immediately north of the Equator, and entirely in 1820. Britain on her part paid £400,000 to compensate for seizure of ships, and 'for the losses which are a necessary consequence of the Abolition of the said Traffic'.

The Spaniards got their bargain because Englishmen were willing to pay others to follow a good example, and it would be hard to find a precedent in European history. In ordinary times £400,000 might not have seemed a large sum: £100,000 had been provided, a few years earlier, to turn Nelson's clerical brother into a landed nobleman, in recognition of Trafalgar: and as Castlereagh told the House, Spanish merchants at Havana had actually offered five times that amount for the privilege of continuing the Trade: but the times were hard, the country was in the middle of a severe post-war depression, and one Member, not unrepresentative, protested that:

If the coffers of the country were full, I should be willing enough to give the noble lord even a million of money if he wanted it; but, now the coffers are empty, we cannot afford unnecessary expenditure, and I am averse to granting 400 pence to any potentate in Europe.

The protest brought Wilberforce to his feet. If the country were really determined to bring about a universal Abolition of the Slave

Trade, he said, the method of bargain was cheaper than that of force. The removal of this obstacle to friendly relations with Spain might well lead to increased trade, he added, and in any case it was right for England, treading a new and difficult path alone, to be generous. She should, in fact, pay for her pleasures, even if these were virtuous. 'Generosity', he said, 'is only justice. Considering the many blessings which the Almighty has showered on this country, it would be shameful to refuse such a sum for so great a purpose.'

There was no further opposition worth speaking of. 'I believe', said one supporter, 'that if you went from house to house, you would have no difficulty in raising a contribution for the purpose of putting down this traffic.' In the upshot, only four votes were cast against the terms of the Treaty, and so by 1818 all the Powers of the Western World had either made the Trade illegal, or had pledged themselves to do so.

And yet—slaving actually increased! The Latin countries, their bribes pocketed, enforced no penalties for defiance of the law, while America, although she made participation in the Trade an act of piracy, punishable with death, was so little able to control her mercantile marine that in the course of a few years it was literally true that of all the flags of the Atlantic nations, the Union Jack alone was no protection to a slaver. Other countries, jealous of Britain's naval strength, long held out against a reciprocal power of search, and even the sustained efforts of Wellington, a man with unique prestige abroad, who by his zeal for the cause made Wilberforce say that he would 'love all generals the better for it for as long as I live', could not bring about a change of heart.

It was becoming clearer with every year that passed that effective Abolition was impossible without Emancipation, a conclusion long held by advocates of the cause. It was unlikely that Wilberforce would be given the time and strength to effect it, but he could make a start.

II

The West Indian planters, by now experienced in the ways of Parliament, were adepts in delay. They had fought long and successfully against Abolition of the Slave Trade; aided by events in

Europe they would fight against the Registration of their slaves every inch of the road. As for Emancipation, they could fend that matter off, with a little luck, for a whole generation. Abolition of the Trade could be—and was—countered by smuggling slaves under foreign flags. Registration could be argued against as interference with the internal affairs of the Islands, while Emancipation—so great a subject, and involving so many other countries—might be trusted to take care of itself, at least for the time. Meanwhile, they could smear. Ramsay had been an early victim. Wilberforce might be another, and that his reputation was not hopelessly blighted already was no fault of their malice and invention. 'If all that was published about me was true', he wrote, 'nothing but a special Providence can have prevented my being hanged thirty years ago.'

Unhappily for the West Indians, Wilberforce was no Ramsay. He was influential; he was resilient; he was incorruptible; and a man had only to meet him face to face, or to have known him even slightly, to realise how ludicrous it was to try to blacken his fame in the eyes of his countrymen. 'I get . . . to be less touchy as to my character', he wrote to Stephen, putting the matter down partly to 'the decay of natural spirits', partly to 'a growing indifference to human estimation'. Unhappily, not all agitators had the same resilience. More than one suffered, if not quite the fate of Ramsay, yet 'serious alarm'.

What could be said on the West Indian side was that many slaves actually believed that they had already been set free by the British Parliament, and believed it was only illegal defiance on the part of their masters which kept them in bondage. As a consequence, they became increasingly insubordinate, and from time to time, as at Barbados in 1816, they combined, refused to work, and did damage to the plantations. Such insurrections were suppressed with extreme severity, with military help, and at the cost of life or great suffering to the slaves.

> They have actually printed and published in the West Indies [said Wilberforce] that the design of the Friends of Abolition was to make all slaves instantly free. Though unable to read, the domestic slaves obtain and promulgate the notion that their friends in Great Britain were labouring to give them liberty, while their masters were the only people

opposed to it. [He added, with all the emphasis of which he was capable] I beg leave to say distinctly that I and my friends are clear of the blood so unhappily shed.

A statement of the truth, on the part of the masters, might have saved disorder and loss. The slaves could have been told that, while the Trade itself had been legally abolished, that was all. Yet since fresh recruits continued to be smuggled in, this would not have answered, so they were told nothing. Naturally, they continued to suspect the worst, and they can scarcely be blamed for so doing.

Wilberforce had a clear conscience about events in the Caribbean, and he became more determined in his outlook than ever. His repudiation of responsibility for what was happening overseas was soon followed by a positive declaration. 'They charge me with fanaticism', he said of his plans. 'If to be feelingly alive to the sufferings of my fellows is to be a fanatic, I am one of the most incurable fanatics ever permitted to be at large.' He gave notice that the cause of the slaves would be carried forward step by step, and he was by now confident of success, 'because the people of England are religious and moral, loving justice and hating iniquity. . . . I rely upon the religion of the people of this country.'

Although he was right so to do, yet steps for relief would still need to be gradual, as in the past. The people of England might love justice, but many of them were themselves in distress, and so, just as Abolition had been held up by events abroad, general Registration of slaves, the first measure towards the new goal, was affected by post-war troubles at home. It was not considered politic, even by some of the 'fanatics' themselves, to press their cause, when so many of what were known as the 'labouring poor' of England were in bitter want. The question was shelved, not forgotten.

> I have for some time [wrote Wilberforce to Zachary Macaulay in 1817] been unwillingly yielding to a secret suggestion that it would be better perhaps to lie upon our oars in the Registry cause. When Parliament meets, the whole nation, depend upon it, will be looking up for relief from its own burthens; and it would betray an ignorance of all tact to talk to them in such circumstances of the sufferings of the slaves in the West Indies. We should specially guard against appearing to have a world of our own, and to have little sympathy with the sufferings of our countrymen.

This letter touches upon a matter cardinal to any consideration of Wilberforce's life and achievement—the continuing contrast between his record at home, consistent in its acceptance of much that was repressive and unjust, though never un-alive to suffering, and his tireless agitation for the relief, cost what it might, of the West Indian Negro. It is a recurring criticism not only of Wilberforce himself but of other members of the Clapham Sect. It is one which cannot be evaded, but the comment made by Mr. E. M. Forster in his study of the people most concerned will find many sympathisers:

> I agree with the line of criticism. But I do not share the moral indignation that sometimes accompanies it. The really bad people, it seems to me, are those who do no good anywhere, and help no one either at home or abroad. There are plenty of them about, and when they are clever as well as selfish they often manage to slip through their lives unnoticed, and to escape the censure of historians.

During the pause in the campaign, evidence accumulated of continuing brutalities towards the slaves. As always, it was the work of a minority of planters, and the instances quoted are important first as showing what *could* occur in slave territory, and then because they helped to reawaken England. In one case a planter ordered two slave boys, accused of receiving a stolen pair of stockings, a hundred lashes apiece, and the sister of one of them thirty lashes for shedding tears when she saw them beaten. On this occasion, the Attorney-General was satisfied that the evidence justified prosecution of the master. A local grand jury rejected this view, and the matter was, in consequence, dropped. The outcry was as loud as it was warranted.

In another case a certain Mr. Rawlins was concerned. He appears to have been in Holy Orders, though manager of an estate at St. Kitts.

A runaway slave was caught and brought back to his plantation in an exhausted state. Next day, he was severely flogged. The day after, he was set to work, chained to another slave. He complained of pain and hunger, and tried to lie down, but he was beaten to his feet, Rawlins then being present. In the course of the day he died, still chained to his fellow.

This time the law could not be wholly evaded. A coroner's jury did their best for Rawlins, their ridiculous verdict being 'Died by the visitation of God.' But Rawlins was tried, on the Attorney-

General's insistence, found guilty of manslaughter, and sent to prison for three months with a fine of £200.

Joseph Marryat, father of the novelist and a powerful man in the West Indies, told the House that the punishment was regarded locally as 'very severe'. The Colonial Secretary, on the other hand, wrote to the appropriate Governor: 'Mr. Rawlins could not have been guilty of manslaughter: it must have been murder or an acquittal.' Rawlins, in fact, was lucky, nearly as lucky in his way as the flogger of the compassionate little girl.

Such cases as these, which darken the entire history of slavery in the West Indies and the Americas, arouse feeling today, just as they did then. And they did more for the cause Wilberforce had at heart than any reasoning. They even moved the local Legislatures, although, as the Attorney-General, Romilly, said in the House, 'those laws which look so well on paper, which appear so well calculated to benefit the slave population, not only are not executed, but were never intended to be executed'. It was, in fact, the Slave Trade evasion over again. Romilly quoted a typical instance from a despatch from a local Governor.

> The Act for encouraging the better government of slaves lately passed in Dominica appears to have been considered, from the day it was passed till this hour, as a political measure—to prevent the interference of the Mother Country in the management of the slaves.

Joseph Marryat used to ask his son, author of the most racy and authentic novels of the Navy of Nelson's era, whether he saw any substantial difference in the way in which the West Indian Negroes and the sailors in King's ships were treated. Young Frederick was sometimes at a loss for an answer. The best would have been that two wrongs do not make a right, and that, judging by the speed of enlightenment in the West Indies, the lot of British seamen would be eased long before the planters' conscience moved them to lighten the misery of their Negroes.

Ultimately, it was their own stupidity which defeated the West Indians. By their continuing obstinacy in defying the laws of the Mother Country in matters of the Slave Trade, and in treatment of their Africans, they caused the Abolitionists to skirt the process of Registration altogether, and to proceed inexorably towards Emancipation.

III

It was often charged against Wilberforce that he did not know exactly what he was doing; that he was a visionary with no understanding of the capabilities, or lack of them, in those he was befriending. It is true that he may have hoped for too much, and that he had not studied, in Africa itself, the background from which the slaves came, but nor had that stern realist, Wellington, and others of the same way of thinking. For most of them the straight issue was contained in the proposition stated by Thomas Jefferson:

> That all men are created equal, that they are endowed by their Creator with certain undeniable Rights, that among these are Life, Liberty and the Pursuit of Happiness.

What Wilberforce did see was at least one instance of a man who, having freed himself from a society in which he had been a chattel, sought help in bringing civilisation to his fellows. This was Christopher, later King of Hayti, with whom Wilberforce had many dealings.

Christopher was born a slave at St. Kitts. By his industry, honesty and capacity he soon raised himself into a position of trust. He came in time to Hayti, where he took a leading part in the rising against the French. Under his leader Toussaint Louverture he learnt something of administration, and he had a principal share in overthrowing Toussaint's too sanguinary successor, Dessalines. Thereupon he assumed the Governorship of the north part of the Island, the south falling to a fellow-officer, Pétion, a mulatto.

In 1807 Christopher devised a Napoleonic constitution by which, as President and Commander-in-Chief for life, he perpetuated his own rule, on the lines of his French model. A few years later, he had himself crowned, with his entire army in attendance. Having read accounts of Napoleon's ceremony with attention, King Henry, as he now styled himself, assumed the crown before allowing it to be bestowed on him by his Protestant 'Archbishop'.

Ceremony and constitution were as far as Henry looked to France. In general, that country was an enemy who might at any time reconquer old territory, and reintroduce slavery to free citizens. It was to England, therefore, that Henry looked for protection and security. On the night of his coronation, with British and American merchants present, he gave the toast of

> My dear Brother George! May his life be preserved by the Great Ruler of the Universe, and may he oppose an invincible obstacle to the unbridled ambition of Napoleon, and remain always the constant friend of Hayti!

But security was not enough. Henry's treasury was full, his army well organised, and he determined to spend lavishly on education. The whole system, he said, must be English, and in his need he turned to Wilberforce.

> He has requested me [wrote Wilberforce to Stephen] to get for him seven schoolmasters, a tutor for his son, and seven different Professors for a Royal College he desires to found. Among these are a classical professor, a medical, a surgical, a mathematical, and a pharmaceutical chemist.

Not only the choice of persons, but, within limits, their salaries were left to Wilberforce's discretion, and the quest involved him in innumerable letters and interviews. 'Much harassed', the diary noted, 'by applications for recommendations to Hayti by people of whom I know nothing.' Stephen, who had lived in the West Indies himself, said that religious zeal and the desire for money were the 'only two motives strong enough to keep any man or woman, without necessity' six months there, and indeed, the candidates who presented themselves were of a mixed kind. Yet the task had its pleasures, even though Wilberforce could not find a man of religion such as he could approve, this being his chief ambition. 'How I wish I was not too old, and you not too busy to go', he wrote to Macaulay. Friends shared his enthusiasm.

> Were I five and twenty [wrote Sir Joseph Banks], as I was when I embarked with Captain Cook, I am very sure I should not lose a day in embarking for Hayti. To see a set of human beings emerging from slavery and making most rapid strides towards the perfection of civilisation, must I think be the most delightful of all food for contemplation.

Banks was then over seventy, and there is no doubt that he was sincere in what he said, and that his sentiment was echoed by many zealots for the cause of human progress. Nor was Wilberforce without practical good sense. To find the right tutor for Henry's son was a matter which could be of supreme importance. Of this appointment Wilberforce said:

> I should prefer a man of sound sense and some knowledge of the world, provided he was really a practical Christian, to any man of great religious zeal who might be likely to push matters further than the state of the King's mind or the circumstances and disposition of the population in general would probably bear.

Nothing was overlooked, right down to ploughmen with their ploughs, four of which he found easily enough. But, Wilberforce confessed:

> My heart quite fails me at the idea of sending those four raw creatures into so distant and to them so strange a clime, without preparing them for what they have to expect.

No more was heard of them, but it is possible that they did as well as the professors, some of whom made good, others of whom quarrelled or took to drink.

A naval officer who visited Hayti described Henry as:

> What in England you would call a fine, portly looking man . . . and on horseback, where he certainly looks his best, he has much the appearance of old George. . . . It is *his* mind that governs all; he has the ablest men of his kingdom employed about his person, but they are mere executors of his will. One proof of his being neither a very changeable nor cruel man is that almost all the great officers of the palace, who were there four years ago, are there now; and they bear, generally speaking, the characters of good and just men. . . . He certainly is bringing that great question to a fair trial—Whether the negroes possess sufficient reasoning powers to govern themselves or, in short, whether they have the same capacities as white men. And he is the only man, I think, in the world, who could have given it so bold a trial.

Alas for hopes! In 1820, a mere two years after the account was written, a group of officers, irked by Henry's rigid discipline, mutinied, with the sympathy of most of the army. The King, deserted and desperate, took his own life.

Many of Henry's aspirations died with him. 'Every day something transpires', wrote one of Wilberforce's most successful choices, 'to show the importance of King Henry to the Haytians. His greatest

16   CHARLES JAMES FOX
From a bust by Joseph Nollekens

17 COMMEMORATIVE
MEDAL, 1807, BY
T. WEBB (obverse)

18 SLAVE IN CHAINS
MEDALLION DESIGNED
BY HACKWOOD FOR
JOSIAH WEDGWOOD,
1786

enemies now acknowledge that they never had a chief whose powers of mind and body were so fitted for command.'

Despite the fact that for some fourteen years Henry had instilled an idea of service, within a framework of political freedom, into those with whom he fought, and whom he later ruled, the failure of so many of his plans gave an excuse for the bitterer unprogressives to say 'I told you so', and to repeat to Wilberforce that no good could ever come of emancipating slaves, since they could not benefit from freedom. Had this opinion been universal, instead of merely common, no progress of any kind would ever have been made among backward people.

Education, and above all political education, is a hard and painful process; but no setback is a valid excuse for not trying. Moreover, had the unprogressives known more history, they would have discovered that, even in what they knew as darkest Africa, there had been civilisations of which the literate world even yet knows little. And Hayti, in spite of Henry's death, remained independent. Her representative is to this day accredited at the Court of St. James.

IV

In May 1821, when three months short of his sixty-second birthday, Wilberforce approached the man he wished to succeed him as leader in the cause of the slaves. He felt that although he himself might have a few more useful years before him in Parliament, yet at the pace at which altruistic legislation proceeded, he could not reasonably hope to carry Emancipation. He wished to ensure that the cause would be taken up by capable hands.

Thomas Fowell Buxton, who was his choice, was a Quaker, born in 1786, and, therefore, with a long expectation of vigour on behalf of any measure he took up. He had hitherto been chiefly interested in Prison Reform, and he sat as Member for Weymouth. Wilberforce had liked him from the first. They had worked and spoken on the same side for reform of the Criminal Laws. Buxton was a grave character. 'He never was a child', said a friend: 'he was a man even when in petticoats'. In politics, he was independent, and in the House he had begun to show the capacity of one who could 'hew a statue out of a rock, but not cut out faces upon cherry stones'.

Buxton was willing. Hitherto he had made no special study of the slavery question, but he was glad to do so. He had already joined the African Institution, and he recalled how his mother had impressed the iniquity of slavery on his youthful mind; how his sister's refusal to eat slave-grown sugar had impressed him even while he laughed at her; and how his prentice efforts as an undergraduate, speaking at Trinity College Dublin in debates, had been in opposition to the Slave Trade. To be chosen by such a man as Wilberforce was in itself an honour. An alliance which the elder man described as 'holy' was formed, and it lasted.

Wilberforce's health was beginning to cause anxiety, and there were whole months during which he was unable to attend Parliament, but now that he had secured the fitting man to follow him, he felt some renewal of energy. In July 1822 he was strong enough to move an Address urging that slavery should be prohibited in the new British settlements in Cape Colony. His speech was notable for its grasp of the *singleness* of Africa.

> The countries which we are now beginning to settle are of very vast extent; but still more, by imperceptible boundaries they communicate with the almost interminable regions of the African Continent. And my object is to secure, throughout that vast continent, the prevalence of true British liberty instead of that deadly and destructive evil which would poison the whole body of the soil and render that prodigious area one wide scene of injustice, cruelty and misery.

It was a thin House which listened to his oratory, but Buxton was there, and he said in after years that it was the best speech he ever heard Wilberforce make.

By this time Wilberforce had left his house at Kensington Gore. Despite the fact that he could hear nightingales in the garden, it had grown too smoky a district for a man susceptible to lung, as well as to long-standing gastric, trouble. He settled for a time at Marden Park, where he worked away with his plans. Marianne Thornton gave one of her inimitable glimpses of Wilberforce about this time, the house full to bursting with family and retainers, Mrs. Wilberforce pleased not to have formal entertaining expected of her, as was often the case in London. There was:

an old butler who they wish would not stay but then he is so attached, and his wife who was a cook but now she is so infirm. All this [noted Marianne] is rather as it should be however, for one rather likes to see him so completely in character and would willingly sit in despair of getting one's plate changed at dinner and hear a chorus of bells all day which nobody answers for the sake of seeing Mr. Wilberforce in his element.

Stephen would have liked to help in the work for the slaves, as had Babington of old; 'but', said Wilberforce, 'my province would be that of driver only . . . and then Mrs. Wilberforce will flog the driver every day if she thinks we do too much . . . and I shall flog myself if we do too little'. So he worked alone, finding the strain severe. 'I am becoming heavy and lumbering', he wrote to Babington, 'and not able at once to start into a canter, as I could twenty years ago. Happily it is a good road, and in the right direction.'

By February 1823 a manifesto was ready: early in March (such was the speed of the times) it was published—a pamphlet of some fifty-odd pages called *An Appeal to the Religion, Injustice, and Humanity of the Inhabitants of the British Empire on Behalf of the Negro Slaves of the West Indies.* Wilberforce's titles were no terser than his speeches, but in this case his matter was condensed, well argued, and effective.

First was an analysis of the conditions of slavery. Then came a rebuttal, with weighty evidence, of the argument that the Colonial Legislatures could themselves be left to improve the conditions of servitude and prepare the way for emancipation. Finally, there was an assurance that the Negroes would not only be more moral and more Christian as free men than as slaves, but would actually work harder. In this last section, hopes had necessarily to take the place of proof, and these hopes, at any rate as regards work, were too often belied. In a tropical climate, as anyone who had lived in one could have assured him, few work harder than they must, and the Negro proved no exception.

Buxton's motion, that the House should take into consideration the state of slavery in the British Colonies, was debated on 15 May 1823. It aroused great interest both in the country at large—from which petitions were beginning to flow to Westminster—and in the

Commons. 'The country takes up our cause surprisingly', noted Wilberforce, and he was pleased with the substance, gravity and assurance of Buxton's speech.

Buxton faced squarely the oldest and most effective argument of the opposition—fear of insurrection. He did not deny that this was real, since, as he said: 'Wherever there is oppression there is danger. . . . The question is how that danger can be avoided. I assume it is to be avoided by giving liberty for slavery, happiness for misery.' And he asked the House whether it was not better to incur risk 'for justice and humanity, for freedom and for the sake of giving happiness to millions hitherto oppressed, than for slavery, cruelty and injustice'.

His concrete proposal, which had been agreed upon by the whole circle of Abolitionists, was to declare the freedom of all children born to slaves after a certain day. It was a plan which had already been applied successfully in the northern part of the United States; it had been introduced in Ceylon, and Sir Hudson Lowe had introduced it at St. Helena. Mention of Lowe gave Buxton an opportunity for a point which has an interest to this day, since studies of Bonaparte's exile have continued to appear ever since.

> Generations yet unborn shall know that on such a day in July Sir Hudson Lowe pronounced that the weather was warm; and that, on such a day in the following December, Bonaparte uttered a conjecture that it would rain in the course of the week. Nothing has escaped the researches of the historian—nothing has been overlooked by the hungry curiosity of the public. Yes! one thing has been; that Sir Hudson Lowe gave the death-blow to slavery in St. Helena.

Buxton then traced the property in slaves back to an act of theft, of kidnapping, a daring excursion into the sacred matter of property. Wisely, he followed it up by a hint of compensation.

> When I say that the planter has no claim against the slave, I do not say that he has no claim against the British nation. If slavery be an injustice, it is an injustice which has been licensed by British law.

His proposals, in addition to that of freedom from birth for children of existing slaves, included giving them a higher status than that of chattels in the eyes of the law, providing religious instruction, enforcing marriage, making Sunday a day of rest, and restraining a master's authority to punish. On this basis he moved the general motion:

> That the state of slavery is repugnant to the principles of the British Constitution and of the Christian Religion: and that it ought to be gradually abolished throughout the British colonies, with as much expedition as may be found consistent with a due regard to the well-being of the parties concerned.

It fell to Canning, the Foreign Secretary, to reply for the Government. His denunciation of the evils of slavery did not lack vigour, but he moved a series of amendments emphasising first the need for 'effectual and decisive measures' to improve the conditions of existing slaves, and he looked forward to ultimate Emancipation as the result of a 'determined and persevering, but at the same time judicious and temperate enforcement of such measures'—when the time should be ripe for it.

Wilberforce followed Canning, and it needed all his Parliamentary experience and skill to decide rightly, and at once, how to reply. 'I never got up more utterly unprepared', he said later, so taken aback had he been by Canning's tactics: 'but, D.G., I believe I hit the point. . . . I thank God I judged rightly that it would not be wise to press for more on that night.'

> After all my right honourable friend has conceded we stand in a new situation . . . we have now an acknowledgement on the part of Government that the grievances of which we complain do exist. We have also the assurance that a remedy shall be applied.

The debate ran with a smoothness which would have been unimaginable when Wilberforce first entered Parliament. Brougham spoke out for Emancipation, in which he was a firm believer, and even Charles Ellis, who put the case for the planters, did not defend the institution of slavery itself. He could only describe it as an unfortunate system in which the planters, through no fault of their own, had been involved. He suggested that Buxton's purpose could best be realised

> by a benign, though insensible revolution in manners, by the encouragement of particular manumissions and the progressive amelioration of the condition of the slaves, till it should slide insensibly into general freedom . . . in short, an Emancipation of which not the slaves but the masters should be willing instruments or authors.

The House did not divide, but there was no pinning Canning down
to immediate measures. 'I say', he repeated, 'I abjure the principal of
perpetual slavery; but I am not prepared now to state in what way
I would set about its abolition.'

Canning's amendment stood—and the slaves waited. Their day
of liberation might be nearer: it had not yet arrived, and there was
no means of telling when it would do so.

V

The next few years were, in fact, times of setback. The firmer the
attitude of the public in England towards slavery, the more obstinate
grew the planters, and the more fractious the slaves. Each of these
attitudes was natural: that of England, because her people were
convinced there was a wrong to right: that of the planters, because
it was they who were being interfered with: that of the slaves,
because they had heard so many rumours, but seen so little done for
their benefit.

The Government, headed at first by Liverpool and later by
Canning, certainly meant business, though the first steps they took
led to nothing but trouble. Canning's resolutions were sent out to
the Governors of the West Indian Institutions, together with a letter
from Lord Bathurst, the Colonial Secretary, urging, as an immediate
measure in compliance with the wishes of Parliament, the abolition
of the flogging of females and the use of the whip in the field. The
move raised a fury of indignation. Pious resolutions were one thing,
active measures another. Jamaica was particularly violent in its
expression. An Address was moved in the island's Assembly for the
removal of Bathurst: other speakers even declared that Jamaica
should end her ancient allegiance to Britain, of which she had been
proud since the days of Oliver Cromwell. A protest was carried
unanimously 'whereby the inhabitants of this once valuable island
(hitherto esteemed the brightest jewel in the British Crown) are
destined to be offered a propitiatory sacrifice at the altar of
fanaticism'.

In Barbados a missionary, suspected of sympathy with Emancipation, had his meeting-house destroyed and was driven from the island.

The worst news of all came from Demerara, in British Guiana, where there was serious trouble. There the Governor, alarmed by the attitude of the planters when he communicated Bathurst's despatch, decided to conceal its contents from the Negroes. As a result, rumour spread from plantation to plantation that the King of England had set them free, and that their masters were suppressing the edict. In some districts, slaves refused to work. Troops were called out: insurgents were tried by court-martial and executed. Five (less lucky than those for whom death had been ordained) received a thousand lashes each. Every planter should have been made to witness this punishment in person, and to declare before the civilised world that he approved of every brutal stroke.

The news from Demerara reached London in distorted form: slaves had risen *en masse*, planters had been murdered wholesale, etc. This was not true, but sections of the popular Press, led by Theodore Hook in *John Bull*, unleashed a wholesale tirade against Wilberforce and his friends. 'One of Hook's paragraphs was sent me the other day' noted Wilberforce, 'with only these three words: "THOU VILE HYPOCRITE".'

Damage had been done—to the slaves. The rumours had achieved their end: the truth, when reported, was not believed: but Canning was not a man to be diverted from his purpose. In March 1824 he laid before Parliament proposals for amelioration in Trinidad, together with a draft Proclamation for issue in the Colonies, referring to the erroneous belief that Emancipation had actually been carried out, and declaring that slaves would be 'undeserving of our protection if they shall fail to render entire submission to the laws as well as dutiful obedience to their masters'.

The proposed measures of amelioration were extensive. A new post was suggested, a 'Protector and Guardian of Slaves', charged with the duty of acting on the slaves' behalf in all major legal proceedings in which he might be involved. The use of the whip was to be prohibited for enforcing labour. The whipping of female slaves was to be forbidden altogether. Licences were to be issued authorising the marriage of slaves, and the separation of husband from wife or parent from child by sale was to be forbidden. Slaves were to be allowed to hold and to dispose of property: and these and other measures were to be enforced by heavy penalties.

Canning explained that the regulations were to be applied to Trinidad, St. Lucia, Demerara and other Colonies which had no legislatures of their own, and where the power of the Crown was unshackled. So far as they went, they were excellent, but as Buxton was quick to point out, Canning had promised, in the previous year, amelioration for *all* slaves in the West Indies, and the proposed Order in Council would apply only to some 35,000 out of a total of 700,000. And not a word was to be said, he noted, even in the Colonies concerned, to suggest that the fact of slavery was not to last for ever.

When Wilberforce rose, it was with something of his former power and persuasiveness:

> The House must not conceal from itself what the grand principle—the practical point at issue—really is: It is simply this—whether the slave system is to be put an end to by the Imperial legislature or by the Colonial assemblies.

As long as Parliament left it to the planters, the slaves would despair of any real relief. In their despair they might take matters into their own hands:

> It is my daily and nightly prayer, it is the hope and desire I feel from the bottom of my soul, that so dreadful an event may not occur. But it is a consequence which I cannot but apprehend, and, as an honest man, it is my duty to state that apprehension. Only consider what a terrible thing it is for men who have long lived in a state of darkness, just when the light beams of day have begun to break in upon their gloom, to have the boon suddenly withdrawn, and to be consigned afresh to darkness, uncertainty, nay, to absolute despair! Whatever Parliament may think fit to do, I implore it to do it quickly and firmly. Do not proceed with hesitating steps. Do not tamper with the feelings you have yourselves excited. . . .

But Canning was not to be moved by eloquence. He had done much already: he would do more. For the time, he was restrained by many considerations. There were still the reactionaries in the Lords, ready to block any general measures, and some of them were in the Government. Again, he had many friends among the West Indian interest, some of them enlightened men whom he did not despair might yet be the means of their own salvation. And as he said: 'If this be not a question requiring deliberation, cautious and fearful deliberation, I know not what can be so.'

The House was with him. The measures, as they then stood, were carried without a division. Shortly after the debate, Wilberforce collapsed with pneumonia, and it was more than two months before he could leave his sick-room.

On 1 June 1824 Wilberforce was once more back in the House of Commons—forced there by indignation at the case of a missionary in Demerara, news of whose trials had reached him, briefly, before his illness.

John Smith, the man concerned, had been involved in the insurrection. He had made many negro converts to Christianity, and he had advised his congregations, in their own interest, to avoid the use of force, when they warned him of impending trouble. When strikes and disorder actually began, Smith, although he had told the manager of a near-by estate that riot might spread, was suspected of complicity. He was arrested and confined in the local gaol. The conditions there were appalling, and for two months Smith's wife voluntarily shared his ordeal.

He had been seized on 21 August. On 13 October he was tried by court-martial, without professional legal aid. The proceedings were an outrageous farce, even in a slave-owning community. Evidence was falsified, and Smith was compelled to testify against himself. He was convicted and sentenced to death. There was, it is true, a formal recommendation to mercy, and this was promptly extended by the Home Government. Some months later, Smith died in prison. His widow was forbidden to attend the funeral, and his enemies even tore up the railings with which two devoted Negroes had surrounded his grave.

Brougham, with the full might of his eloquence and legal knowledge, denounced the trial as 'a violation of law and justice'. Wilberforce also spoke, though under great strain. 'I quite forgot my topics', his diary noted pathetically, 'and made sad work of it.' Nothing was done beyond ventilating the whole matter, and the decline of his powers led Wilberforce to wonder if he had not better 'give up taking part in the House of Commons'. He nerved himself for one more speech, which he delivered on 15 June, when

presenting a petition from the town of Carlow in favour of the
Abolition of slavery. This speech took a familiar course:

> I am disposed to think [he said, addressing himself to Canning] that
> my right honourable friend deceives himself as to the probable conduct
> of the West Indian assemblies by insensibly admitting the persuasion
> that the West Indian proprietors in this country—many of whom are
> his own personal friends and men of the most humane and liberal
> minds—reflect the opinions and feelings of the colonists actually in the
> islands. Nothing, alas! could be more different. . . . The West Indians
> abhor alike the end we have in view and the means by which we hope
> to attain it. They frankly tell us that the Emancipation of their slaves
> will be their inevitable destruction; and their prejudices make them
> disapprove of the various measures we recommend for the improve-
> ment of the negroes' condition. . . . When both means and end are like
> obnoxious, it seems to me far too sanguine to look to their giving up
> their opposition and at length adopting the principles we recommend. . . .
> But only let the Imperial Legislature assume its proper tone and main-
> tain its just authority, and all will go on quietly: you will soon witness
> with delight the accomplishment of your benevolent purpose. . . .

Every word was true, and much of it was prophetic: but the slaves
had to wait two more years for Emancipation, and Wilberforce's
work would be continued by other hands than his own. He was now
feeble. He had given his last strength to the cause he had fostered in
Parliament since 1787. Ten days after the debate he was taken ill
again, and for a month lay in a critical condition. He could not know
it, but his work was not far from being achieved. The pattern of
recent events would repeat itself with gathering momentum, and in
the end, right would triumph and the slaves be freed. Wilberforce
even lived to hear, on his death-bed, that the measure he desired had
been carried, though the wider struggle against the exploitation of
the African took up the greater part of the nineteenth century, so
little did other nations share this country's zest in the humanitarian
cause.

God had once more blessed His servant.

7 THE MAN IN PERSON

AFTER the year 1825, Wilberforce's frail, diminutive figure was seen no more at Westminster. With him vanished the last of the great figures of the golden age of oratory. 'When Mr. Wilberforce passes through the crowd', so a foreign observer had remarked on the day of the opening of Parliament, 'everyone contemplates this little man, worn with age and with his head sunk upon his shoulders, as a sacred relic—as the Washington of humanity.'

One eye saw him in a gayer aspect, not the less affectionately. Soon after he had recovered from the illness that was to cause his resignation, Wilberforce suddenly appeared on a visit to his beloved Battersea Rise. Marianne Thornton, then a young lady grown to dignity and capability, was there to greet him with the rest of her family. Neither Wilberforce nor she were in a stage of life to run races together on the lawn, but that was where the old man still liked to be:

> And he was strong enough to spend almost the whole morning walking upon the grass, inhaling as he said the Gales of Roses and listening to the concerts of nightingales. He looks very thin and reduced and walks feebly but really he is almost a proof already of the immortality of the soul—for I never saw him in such spirits or appear so keenly *active* upon all subjects. He explained it by saying they had begun to feed him with raw beef again, and that he was so *animated* and exhilarated he hardly knew how to keep within due bounds: and perhaps the degree of comparative quiet in which they now keep him makes him enter with

more spirit and soul on the subjects on which he *does* dwell—I wish you could have seen him as he stood under the Tulip Tree telling of . . . many of whom he has seen pass and re-pass amongst our shades—'and they are gone—and here am I—' he said, 'a wreck left for the next tide —but yet abounding in blessings and enjoyments'.

'Blessings and enjoyments'—the words were always on Wilberforce's lips, and it was the desire that others should share them that had been the driving force of his life. Marianne's 'They', those who looked after him, were his wife, his sons and his second daughter, Elizabeth, for Barbara, his elder girl had died in 1821. As Elizabeth herself was frail, it would be to his sons that he would turn increasingly not so much for comfort (which he was still able to give as much as to receive) but for help in such work as he still undertook, and as sharing in his religion, his enthusiasms, which included the principal missionary societies, and his pursuits.

The visit to Battersea took place after a protracted stay at Bath, where at first he had lived quietly, but where his activity gradually increased, till it began to resemble the state of affairs which his social gifts always attracted.

> There is walking between the glasses and after the glasses [so he wrote to his surviving daughter about 'taking the waters'] and then in rolls the tide of visitors as regularly as that of the ocean; and, like that, this human influx makes its way through and over every obstacle. . . . Continued knockings which I hear when writing, and at last one intruder has actually made a lodgement.

At Bath, he was not far from Hannah More, and the two could foregather. 'Sat with Hannah More about an hour and a half', he recorded, 'and she as animated as ever I knew her, quoting authors, naming people, etc.—Off about one, after praying with her.' Hannah was in fact fourteen years older than Wilberforce. She was then a vigorous woman of eighty, an age which Wilberforce never reached.

When Canning knew that he was to retire, he saw to it that Wilberforce was offered a peerage, which would have enabled him to speak, when he so wished, on public affairs. Wilberforce had never regretted that the plan to ennoble him had come to nothing in Pitt's day. Now, he said courteously, declining the suggestion, 'I have done nothing to make it naturally come to me.' He preferred to remain a private citizen, even though he would never be an unknown one.

After his interval at Bath, he bought a house, Highwood Hill, 'about ten miles north of London'. It was at Mill Hill, where his friends thought he might be persuaded to settle. 'I shall be a little *zemindar* there', he said, '140 acres of land, cottage of my own etc.' For a time it looked as if it might be so, particularly as his eldest son, William, proposed to farm.

Marianne Thornton was among the earlier and most welcome visitors, and her description was as amusing as ever:

> Many dinner bells ringing but no dinner. Dissenting ministers ringing the door bell because they heard the dinner bells, the house a collection of rabbit hutches containing two married sons and their families, the blind secretary and his family, the deaf butler and his, and the secretary who *could* see could not find a book which was required, or even feel that it was his duty to find it.

Disintegration might be setting in—but not devitalisation. Out in the fields, William was dairy-farming. Marianne had never liked him, and her comment was: 'I wish William would keep company with his father instead of his cows. It would be quite as profitable and much more agreeable.' She guessed that William would be a poor farmer.

Two years later, Marianne went again to Highwood, and a description she composed on this visit is one of the most revealing she ever wrote. Family prayers had always been a feature with the Wilberforces, as they were in the houses of all the Clapham Sect:

> The scene at prayers is a most curious one. There is a bell which rings when Mr. Wilberforce begins to dress; another when he finishes dressing; upon which Mr. Barningham begins to play a hymn upon the organ and sing a solo, and by degrees the family come down to the entrance hall where the psalmody goes on; first one joins in and then another; Lizzy calling out: 'Don't go near Mama, she sings so dreadfully out of tune, dear' and William: 'Don't look at Papa, he does make such dreadful faces.' So he does, waving his arms about and occasionally pulling the leaves of the geraniums and smelling them, singing out louder and louder in a tone of hilarity. 'Trust Him, praise Him, trust Him, praise Him ever more.' Sometimes he exclaims 'Astonishing! How very affecting! Only think of Abraham, a fine old man, just a kind

of man one should pull off one's hat to, with long grey hairs, and looking like an old aloe—but you don't know what an aloe is perhaps: it's a tree, no a plant which flowers . . .' and he wanders off into a description about plants and flowers.

Marianne, had she written the old man's life, would have done it inimitably. As it was, when, in due time, she heard that Robert and Samuel, the second and third sons, were setting about it—she sighed. She thought that, however devoted, such men could never properly 'appreciate that winged being and all his airy flight—why you might as well put a mole to talk about an eagle'.

II

Marianne Thornton's likening of Wilberforce to an eagle was less apt than was her habit. An eagle is solitary: Wilberforce was otherwise. Considering the qualities of his voice, admired both in singing and speaking, and his sweetness, a nightingale would perhaps have been a closer comparison. 'Of all the men I know', said Pitt, 'Wilberforce has the greatest natural eloquence.' Pitt was a good judge, and his opinion has not been disputed. This quality, and his 'delight in little things, the buoyant youth surviving in the man' were what struck everyone who knew him.

Wilberforce's religion was of the proselytising kind, and, had he been a different kind of person, it would have made him a bore. His note-books were full of jottings as to how he could 'get at' his less serious friends, and there is a story of an old peer he once visited on a sick-bed. Wilberforce studiously kept off religion, but when someone else came into the room and asked the invalid how he was getting on, he said, 'Well enough, considering Wilberforce sitting here telling me I am going to Hell.'

This story is reminiscent of another, preserved in the writer's own family. They did not love Wilberforce, since they were pioneers in the West Indies, and, although humane and liberal in their out-look, suffered much, materially, from his campaigns. Wilberforce, so this story runs, was once at a winter meeting of a missionary society, and he told them he had dreamt that he was in Hell. 'It was just like here', he added thoughtfully, almost to himself: 'I could not get near the fire for parsons.'

True or not, this was the sort of remark which enchanted Madame de Staël, who once said that 'Mr. Wilberforce is the best converser I have met with in this country. I have always heard that he was the most religious, but now I find that he is the wittiest man in England.' He was, so she said and so others agreed, completely 'amusable'. 'I expected from him all that was elevated in instruction', said Fanny Burney, 'but there was a mixture of simplicity and vivacity in his manner that I had not expected, and found really captivating.'

Wilberforce often shrank, when it came to the point, from inflicting his religious views on his more worldly friends. It was otherwise with letters. 'It is of great importance to preserve boys affections, and prevent their thinking home a dull place', he wrote with wisdom, but he never shirked the task—it was not a burden —of writing them long letters about their spiritual condition. So far from resenting them, these screeds were carefully, even reverently preserved.

It was the same with his mother. In her later years (she died in 1798), her character modified, and from delight in worldly pleasures, she turned increasingly to religion. All the same, it was an unusual relationship which could admit that a newly-married man of under forty should write, as Wilberforce did in September 1797:

> I trust my dear mother rather gains than loses ground; I need hardly say that I remember you daily in my prayers. May you, my dearest mother, learn to be at the same time conscious of your own demerits as a sinner, and of the mercy and love of God, who holds out promises of pardon and acceptance to all penitent believers in Christ. May you learn more habitually to look to the Holy Spirit of God for all necessary supplies of grace and consolation; for a more melting penitence; for a strengthened faith; for a more animated hope; and a more perfect love and acquiescence in the Divine will concerning you.
>
> May you be enabled, my dearest mother, more constantly to retain a practical impression of that which we all believe and know, and that the daily trials to which we are subjected, be they greater or smaller, do not happen to us by chance, but that they, as well as more important events, are the ordination of that gracious Being, who does not willingly afflict the children of men, and who has promised that all things shall work together for good to them that love Him. Thus, while your outward man decays, may your inward man be renewed day by day;

and may your present sufferings, though while they last wearisome and
grievous, serve to minister to you in the end, a more abundant entrance
into the everlasting Kingdom of God. I make no apologies for writing
to you is this style, because I am persuaded that you prefer it to any
other. Alas! It is much easier to advise others, than to put in practice
your own advice.

This letter, written so obviously by a lay preacher, the Parliamentary
orator, and the author of the then recently published, *Practical View
of the Prevailing Religious System of Professed Christians* . . . is quoted
because it is as typical as it was sincere. The wheel had indeed come
full circle, and that old Mrs. Wilberforce—once so concerned at her
son's solemnity—affectionately preserved the sermon, shows that it
was neither resented, nor, as it could have been, misunderstood.

With Wilberforce's unhesitating assumption of the preaching
role, it is not without interest to note the type of cleric of whom he
approved. His judgment was severe, but some passed the test—
Wesley, Newton and Milner, pre-eminently. Milner, to whom he
owed his own conversion, died in 1820 under Wilberforce's own
roof at Kensington Gore. 'Never was there an easier dismission',
he noted, 'which is the more observable because he had fears of
the pain of dying: when he was told he was in danger, he grew
more composed and calm than he had been before.' Milner,
in his last hours, as in his strength, proved an example to his
friend.

Other clergymen met with scrutiny which, if never unkindly,
was often sharp. For instance, when Wilberforce was in company
with Dean Ryder of Wells, a certain 'Dr. W.' was introduced. 'The
true picture', so Wilberforce noted, 'of a sensible, well-informed and
educated, polished, old, well-beneficed, nobleman's and gentleman's
house-frequenting, literary and chess-playing divine—of the best
sort. . . . I hope beginning to be serious.' There is not much doubt
that the man observed so closely was Richard Warner, author of
popular works on Bath and its district, in his day a celebrity. And at
least one bishop, Gloucester, answered all requirements. He, noted
Wilberforce in 1819, 'is really what a bishop should be—for
humility, industry, zeal with sobriety, hospitality, and above all,
for love in all its kinds and directions, he is really a bright specimen;
and the veneration and affection that are felt for him by all who know

19   THE WILBERFORCE FAMILY BIBLE, WITH ENTRIES IN WILBERFORCE'S OWN HAND.
NOW AT HULL

20   MONUMENT TO WILBERFORCE

From the statue (1840) by Samuel Joseph in Westminster Abbey

him, even by those who do not entirely concur with him in religious principles, are seen beaming from every countenance, and sparking in every eye.'

III

Wilberforce, with his short sight, was no connoisseur of the arts. He knew and sat to various painters, but there is no indication that he took more than a perfunctory interest in their work, and he was certainly not a collector. With literature it was otherwise. He was an incessant reader, nurtured, like so many great Parliamentarians, on the Greek and Latin Classics, and keeping acquaintance with them all through life. He was able to converse at ease in French; and his mind was stored with the Bible, with Shakespeare, and with his beloved Cowper. 'Walked from Hyde Park Corner, repeating the 119th Psalm in great comfort', he noted in 1820, and his pockets were always stuffed with solid reading matter. Of the younger men, he liked Wordsworth—'very manly, sensible and full of knowledge', so he thought him, 'but independent almost to rudeness'.

Another writer, Southey, provided the perfect instance of Wilberforce's effect upon a stranger. 'Battersea Rise', noted Wilberforce's diary on 26 April 1817, 'to dinner, where Southey. Saw him for the first time, and much struck with him. Acland, Lord Sidmouth, Robert Grant, Governor Raffles etc. We dined at seven o'clock, and time flew away so rapidly, that we kept on chatting till two in the morning, and my watch having stopped, thought it was half-past eleven.'

Southey, on his part, wrote an account of the same occasion to Wilberforce's sons:

> It was at Battersea Rise that I saw Mr. Wilberforce for the first time. A memorable day it was to me. How it happened I know not, but although no person can be more disinclined to disputation than myself, we got into one upon the question of Catholic Emancipation; your father and Sir Thomas Acland taking the one side, and I the other. . . . It was a subject on which I spoke with no diffidence, because nothing could appear to me more certain than the perilous consequences which would ensue if the friends of the Church should be so far deluded by its enemies, as to assist them in throwing down the bulwarks of the Protestant establishment.

But if my temper had been likely to hurry me into any unbecoming warmth, your father's manner would effectively have repressed it. His views, when I thought him most mistaken, were so benign, he took the ground of expediency with so religious a feeling, and argued with such manly yet such earnest sincerity, that if it had been possible to have persuaded me out of an opinion so deeply and firmly rooted, he would have done it. Our discussion, for so it may be called, was protracted till two in the morning.

It was the old story. Strangers, some of them prejudiced either on religious, or slaving or some other grounds, had but to meet Wilberforce face to face, and they were conquered. There is no exception recorded, even among political opponents.

A year later, Southey resumed the acquaintance at Keswick:

I saw more of your father then than at any other time, and certainly I never saw any other man who seemed to enjoy such a perpetual serenity and sunshine of spirits. In conversing with him you felt assured that there was no guile in him; that if ever there was a good and happy man on earth, he was one; and that eminently blessed as he was with a benign and easy disposition, the crown of all his blessings was that inward and undisturbed peace which passeth all understanding.

Marianne Thornton had noted the strangeness of Wilberforce's entourage; so did Southey:

I recollect one circumstance during his visit to the Lakes, which shows the perfect reliance his servants had upon his good nature—forbearance it might be called in any other person, but in him it was no effort. The coachman came in to say that some provision concerning the horses had been neglected, and your father, with a little start of surprise, replied that indeed he had not thought of it. 'No', said the coachman. 'Since you have been in this county, you have all been so lake, and valley, and river, and mountain mad, that you have thought of nothing that you ought to have thought of.'

This was the coachman who led Wilberforce to say, when he met with bad temper in the housekeeper of a friend with whom he was staying: 'You know the Indians have a way of getting oddly contrasted animals to fight with each other, and I really long to set our old coachman and this fine lady in single combat.'

It was not blindness, or lack of knowledge that led Wilberforce to tolerate such idiosyncrasy, but genuine tolerance and understanding. He was not incapable of reproach, but it was motive he looked for, and among those who surrounded him he found the motives good.

And if Wilberforce charmed, he was also susceptible to charm, as in the case of the Prince Regent, always at his best in matters of tact and taste. In 1815 the Prince was at Brighton, enjoying the amenities of his 'Chinese Marine Pavilion', which Wilberforce described as 'beautiful and tasty, though it looks very much as if St. Paul's had come down to the sea and left behind a litter of cupolas'. Wilberforce attended a reception. 'The Prince came up to me,' he said, 'and reminded me of my singing at the Duchess of Devonshire's ball in 1782, of the particular song, and of our then first knowing each other.' Royalty had inherited that memory for details characteristic of the Hanoverians.

'We are both, I trust, much altered since, Sir,' said Wilberforce. 'Yes,' said the Prince, 'the time which has gone by must have made a great alteration in us.' 'Something better than that too, I trust, Sir,' Wilberforce pursued.

The Prince then asked his guest to dine next day, assuring him that he should hear nothing under his roof which would give him pain. Wilberforce obeyed the request, and afterwards said: 'Had I been covered with titles and ribands, I could not have been treated with more real, unaffected, unapparently condescending and therefore more unostentatious civility.'

There is even a glimpse of Wilberforce with the rising generation of royalty. 'In consequence of a very civil message from the Duchess of Kent', he noted in 1820, 'I waited on her this morning. She received me with her fine animated child on the floor with its playthings, of which I soon became one.' Such a glimpse of the old Abolitionist, and the child who was to become Queen Victoria, would have appealed to many historical painters of her reign.

IV

Wilberforce, always insistent that a man should count his blessings, set a good example. One day, he found himself locked up in a committee room in the House during a division, with a man of fashion whom he had lost sight of for many years, and who had just returned to the Commons. He was clearly rather embarrassed. 'You and I, my lord, were pretty well acquainted formerly', said Wilberforce unaffectedly. 'Alas' was the reply, and then (with a deep sigh), 'you and I are a great many years older now'. 'Yes, we are', said Wilberforce, 'and for my part I can truly say that I do not regret it.' '*Don't* you', said the acquaintance, with what Wilberforce described as 'an eager and almost incredulous voice, and a look of wondering dejection, which I never forgot'.

It was in similarly fortuitous circumstances, which might have caused awkwardness, that he encountered Lord Melville, long after Melville's retirement from public affairs.

> We did not meet for a long time [said Wilberforce], and all his connections most violently abused me. About a year before he died, we met in the stone passage which leads from the Horse Guards to the Treasury. We suddenly came upon each other, just in the open part where the light struck upon our faces. We saw one another, and at first I thought he was passing on, but he stopped and called out, 'Ah, Wilberforce, how do you do?' and gave me a hearty shake by the hand. I would have given a thousand pounds for that shake. I never saw him again.

That was the sort of response evoked by the meeting of two generous natures. Where he himself alone was concerned, Wilberforce could be severe and exact in survey.

> When I look back on my past life [he wrote in 1821] and review it, comparing especially the almost innumerable instances of God's kindness to me with my unworthy returns, I am overwhelmed. The exceeding goodness of God to me, and the almost unequalled advantages I have enjoyed, fill me with humiliation.
>
> My days appear few when I look back, but they have been anything but evil. My blessings have been of every kind, and of long continuance; general to me and to other Englishmen, but still more peculiar, from my having a kindly natural temper, a plentiful fortune; all the mercies of my public life, my coming so early into Parliament for Hull, then for Yorkshire. . . . and only ceasing to be M.P. for Yorkshire because I resigned. Then my having been made the instrument of bringing forward the Abolition; my helping powerfully the cause of Christianity in India; my never having been discredited. . . .
>
> Then all my domestic blessings. Marrying as late as thirty-six, yet finding one of the most affectionate of wives; children, all of them

attached to me beyond measure. Then my social blessings. No man ever had so many kind friends; they quite overwhelm me with their goodness. Then my having faculties sufficient to make me responsible—a natural faculty for public speaking. Then, almost above all, my having been rendered the instrument of much spiritual good by my work on Christianity. How many have communicated to me that it was the means of their turning to God.

Praise the Lord, O my soul!

It is one thing to be blessed, another to know it, and to value it without the spur of contrast. Yet Wilberforce was even granted this. His second daughter died in 1831, after a brief married life, and this was a heavy blow to him. Then, through his son William and his experiments in farming, he lost a great part of his capital. Marianne had been right, the 'cow-keeping', as she called it, proved disastrous, and a kindly father paid the bill.

Wilberforce's trouble, when it became known, was the occasion for touching acts of kindness. Several men of fortune, among them Lord FitzWilliam, an old political opponent in Yorkshire, offered, with the greatest tact, to make up all his loss. Wilberforce would accept nothing, except enough to complete the building of a Chapel-of-Ease which he had begun at Mill Hill. His clerical sons were by then beneficed, and it was their pleasure, and his, that he and his wife should live with them, and encourage their pastoral ministrations. 'He is behaving beautifully, they all say', wrote Marianne when Wilberforce sold Highwood, 'as one might be so certain he would.'

V

As if to round off a life, so much of which had been spent at the seat of Government, Wilberforce's last illness occurred in London, at the house of his cousin, Mrs. Lucy Smith. This was in Cadogan Place, not a mile from where his successors at Westminster were settling details of the Bill for the Abolition of Slavery in British possessions. 'I am like a clock that is almost run down', he said to one of the friends who hastened to his side. He was not old as the world today reckons it, being just short of seventy-four, but he had long since told Lord Muncaster: 'I account myself ten years older than most men of my own age', so severely had work drawn upon his resources.

'I am in a very distressed state,' he said to his son Henry, the day before he died. 'Yes', was the reply, 'but you have your feet on the Rock.' 'I do not venture to speak so positively', said the old man, 'but I hope I have.' They were his last words. He died on 30 July 1833, and his passing was the occasion of universal tributes.

> The picture which the dead leave on the minds of their survivors is not always lively or distinct [said John Gurney], but no one who has been accustomed to observe Wilberforce will ever find the slightest difficulty in picturing him on the tablet of the mind.
>
> Who that knew him can fail to recall the rapid movements of his somewhat diminutive form, the illumination of his expressive countenance, and the nimble fingers with which he used to seize on any little object which happened to adorn or diversify his path? Much less can we forget his vivacious wit—so playful, yet so harmless; the glow of his affections; the urbanity of his manners; and the wondrous celerity with which he was ever wont to turn from one bright light to another. Above all, however, his friends will never cease to remember that peculiar sunshine which he threw over a company by the influence of a mind perpetually turned to love and praise.

By the unanimous wish of Parliament, Wilberforce was buried in Westminster Abbey, his coffin followed by immense crowds. His body lies near those of Pitt and Fox.

> He was an enthusiast who was always wise [wrote G. M. Trevelyan in his *English Social History*]. He was an agitator who always retained his powerful gift of social charm, the outcome of his sweet disposition. He is the classic example of the use of the cross-bench politician in our two-party public life. He could not have done what he did if he had desired office. With his talents and position he would probably have been Pitt's successor as Prime Minister if he had preferred party to mankind. His sacrifice of one kind of fame and power gave him another and a nobler title to remembrance.

SOURCES

THE essential basis for a study of Wilberforce is the *Life* by his sons Robert and Samuel, 5 vols. (1838), usefully condensed by Samuel in 1868 into a single volume. The *Correspondence*, 2 vols. (1840), was also published by his sons. The *Private Papers* (1897) are an important supplement, and contain Wilberforce's assessment of Pitt.

Other sources include Gurney's *Familiar Sketch of Wilberforce* (1838); James Stephen's *Essays in Ecclesiastical Biography* (1838); Harford's *Recollections* (1865); Colquhoun's *Wilberforce, His Friends and His Times* (1866); Stoughton's *William Wilberforce*, and a number of shorter works. Incomparably the finest twentieth-century study, one which includes references to the principal literature of the Slave Trade, is Sir Richard Coupland's *Wilberforce: a Narrative* (1923) to which the present venture owes a debt thankfully acknowledged, There is also much to be learnt from Christopher Lloyd's *The Navy and the Slave Trade* (1949) a study based on original research. I am also most grateful to Mrs. Geoffrey Pilkington for the loan of material on Liverpool.

Of more recent publications, Mr. E. M. Forster's *Marianne Thornton* (1956), though talking of Wilberforce only incidentally, gives a proper idea of those who made up the Clapham Sect, and is an example of how to write about people. I am most grateful to him for allowing me to quote so often from it. When the big filial *Life* was preparing, Marianne Thornton wrote: 'I wish . . . I were rich enough to buy up their father's life and burn it, out of love for the great old man'—and indeed it is no work of art. On the other hand, as Sir Reginald Coupland found, by including all the best of Wilberforce's diary, it omitted nothing essential, and it has allowed all succeeding writers to present Wilberforce in his own image.

Everyone attracted to the Abolitionist would find a visit to Hull rewarding. Wilberforce's birthplace is his memorial: his statue, on a tall column, overlooks part of the town; and a delightful small museum in Pickering Park, given to the northern whaling, shows from what activities the prosperity of Hull once derived.

INDEX

The numerals in **bold** type refer to the figure-numbers of the illustrations

This book is due for return on or before the last date shown below.

20. MA 97

0 0 SEP 20

Don Gresswell Ltd.,